THE ANXIOUS ATTACHMENT RECOVERY WORKBOOK

7 PROVEN STEPS TO FEEL DEEPLY LOVED, CHOSEN & SECURE IN JUST 15 MINUTES A DAY

ANDREI NEDELCU

TABLE OF CONTENTS

INTRODUCTION

Imagine you're curled up on your couch, phone in hand, thumb hovering over the screen. Your partner hasn't replied to your last message, sent over an hour ago. You can see they've been online. Your heart races, your palms sweat, and your mind spins with possibilities. Are they ignoring you? Did you say something wrong? Maybe they're talking to someone else—someone more interesting, more attractive, more worthy of their time. You type out another message, delete it, and type again. Should you call? No, that might seem too needy. But if you don't reach out, they might think you don't care. The anxiety builds, a knot in your stomach tightening with each passing minute.

If this scenario feels painfully familiar, you're not alone. Many people experience this kind of intense anxiety in their relationships. You might find yourself constantly seeking reassurance, overanalyzing every interaction, or feeling an overwhelming fear of abandonment. These are all signs of what psychologists call "anxious attachment."

Living with anxious attachment can feel like being on an emotional rollercoaster. One moment, you're flying high on love and connection. The next, you're plummeting into a pit of fear and insecurity. It's exhausting, isn't it? You might wonder why you can't just relax and enjoy your relationships like other people seem to do. Why do you always feel like you're one step away from losing everything?

Anxious attachment isn't a personal flaw or a choice you've made. It's not a sign of weakness or neediness, though it might feel that way sometimes. Instead, it's a pattern of thinking and behaving that developed over time, often rooted in early childhood experiences. Understanding this can be incredibly freeing. It means that with the right tools and support, you can change these patterns and build healthier, more fulfilling relationships.

That's exactly what this book is about. We're going to dive deep into the world of anxious attachment, exploring where it comes from, how it affects your life, and most importantly, how you can start to heal. We'll look at real-life examples that you might relate to and provide practical strategies you can start using right away.

Before we go further, let's take a moment to understand what attachment really means. At its core, attachment is about our need for connection and security in relationships. It's a fundamental human need, as essential as food or water. We're hardwired to form attachments with our caregivers since birth. The quality of these early attachments shapes how we view ourselves, others, and relationships in general.

For those with anxious attachment, these early experiences often involved inconsistent care or attention. Maybe your parents were sometimes warm and attentive, but other times distant or preoccupied. Or perhaps you experienced a significant loss or separation in childhood. As a result, you learned that love and care were unpredictable, leading to a deep-seated fear of abandonment and a constant need for reassurance.

Now, as an adult, these patterns play out in your romantic relationships, friendships, and even work relationships. You might find yourself

- constantly worried about your partner's feelings for you.

- needing frequent reassurance and validation.

- feeling intensely jealous or possessive.

- depending too much on your partner.

- feeling unworthy and having low self-esteem.

- overanalyzing every interaction and reading into things too much.

- having difficulty trusting others.

- feeling like you're "too much" or "not enough."

If these experiences resonate with you, know that you're not broken or unlovable. Your anxious attachment developed as a way to protect yourself and get your needs met in challenging circumstances. It was adaptive then, but now it might be holding you back from the deep, secure connections you truly desire.

The good news is that attachment styles can change. Our brains have an incredible capacity for growth and rewiring, a quality known as neuroplasticity. This means that with consistent effort and the right strategies, you can develop a more secure attachment style. You can learn to trust more easily, to soothe your own anxieties, and to build relationships based on mutual respect and understanding rather than fear and insecurity.

In this book, we'll guide you through this transformative journey. Here's what you can expect:

We'll delve deeper into the science of attachment. You'll learn about the different attachment styles and how they develop. Understanding the "why" behind your anxious attachment can be incredibly empowering and is the first step toward change.

We'll also explore how anxious attachment manifests in your daily life and relationships. We'll look at common patterns and behaviors, helping you identify your own triggers and reactions. This self-awareness is crucial for making lasting changes.

Then, we'll dive into practical strategies for managing anxious thoughts and behaviors. You'll learn techniques for self-soothing, grounding yourself in the present moment, and challenging negative thought patterns. These tools will help you navigate those moments of intense anxiety with more ease and confidence.

We'll also focus on building self-esteem and setting healthy boundaries—two crucial elements for any secure relationship. Many people with anxious attachment struggle with feelings of unworthiness and have difficulty setting limits with others. We'll work on cultivating a stronger sense of self-worth and learning to communicate your needs and boundaries effectively.

Communication is often a major challenge for those with anxious attachment. You might find yourself holding back for fear of pushing others away, or you might overwhelm others with your need for reassurance. We'll explore how to express your needs clearly and effectively, how to listen actively, and how to navigate conflicts in a healthy way.

For those of you who are single or dating, we'll cover how to navigate the dating world with your new understanding of attachment. You'll learn how to recognize secure partners, how to pace new relationships in a healthy way, and how to maintain your sense of self while opening up to love.

We'll also discuss the importance of self-care and building a fulfilling life outside of your romantic relationships. Many people with anxious attachment tend to make their partner the center of their world, which can put immense pressure on the relationship. We'll explore how to cultivate friendships, pursue passions, and create a life that feels meaningful and complete, with or without a romantic partner.

This book isn't about completely eliminating anxiety from your life. Some level of anxiety is normal and even helpful in relationships. It can signal when something needs attention or when our boundaries are being crossed. Our goal is to help you manage your anxiety so it doesn't control your life or your relationships. We want to help you move from a place of constant fear and insecurity to one of general trust and security, with the tools to handle anxiety when it does arise.

Healing is a journey, not a destination. There will be ups and downs, steps forward and steps back. That's okay. Every step you take, no matter how small, is moving you in the right direction. Be patient and compassionate with yourself along the way. Changing long-standing patterns takes time, but it is absolutely possible.

You don't have to do it alone. This book is here to guide you, support you, and remind you that you're capable of forming secure, loving relationships. Many people have walked this path before you and have successfully moved from anxious to secure attachment. Their stories of transformation will inspire you throughout this book.

Are you ready to start understanding and healing your anxious attachment? To build more fulfilling relationships and a more confident you? To break free from the cycle of anxiety and insecurity and step into a life of greater peace and connection? Then let's begin this journey together. Turn the page and take your first step toward secure attachment and healthier relationships. Let's write this new and exciting chapter in your life together.

PART 1

EXPLORING ANXIOUS ATTACHMENT

WHY WE LOVE THE WAY WE DO: THE SCIENCE OF ATTACHMENT

As Emma settled into the chair across from me, I could practically see the worry radiating off her. Her fingers fidgeted with the hem of her shirt, a habit I'd noticed whenever she was particularly anxious. "So, how has your week been?" I asked, already having a hunch about what was coming. Emma sighed, launching into the story of her latest panic over Jake's brief silence. As she spoke, I found myself nodding along. How many times had I seen this scene play out, not just in my office but in my own life and those of friends?

"I knew I shouldn't have sent those texts," Emma groaned, covering her face with her hands. "I'm such a mess."

"Hey, now," I said gently. "You're not a mess. You're human. We've all been there, trust me." I shared a quick story about a time I'd found myself obsessively checking my phone after a date, just to show her she wasn't alone. As we dug deeper into Emma's feelings, I was struck by how universal her fears were. Who hasn't felt that knot in their stomach when someone important doesn't respond right away? The difference was in how consuming these fears had become for Emma.

"It's like… I can't relax unless I know exactly where I stand with Jake," Emma explained, her voice cracking a little. "But then I worry that I'm too needy, and it'll push him away. I just can't win." I leaned forward, my heart going out to her. "Emma, what you're describing is something a lot of people struggle with. We call it anxious attachment, but really, it's just a fancy term for feeling really scared of losing someone you care about."

We spent the rest of the session talking through some ways Emma could handle these feelings. We practiced a simple breathing exercise she could use when anxiety struck and even role-played how she might talk to Jake about her needs without feeling like she was being "too much." As our time wrapped up, I saw a little spark of hope in Emma's eyes. "This isn't going to be a quick fix," I reminded her, "but you're already making progress just by being here and talking about it."

After Emma left, I sat back in my chair, thinking about our session. It's a universal human desire to feel secure in our relationships, but for some of us, it's a tougher road to get there. I made a few notes in Emma's file, already planning for our next session. We'd dive more into her past experiences and work on building up her self-esteem. For now, I hoped she left feeling a little less alone in her struggles. After all, isn't that what we all want? To know that our fears and insecurities don't make us weird or broken, but simply human? As I prepared for my next client, I couldn't help but feel grateful for the work I do. Helping people like Emma navigate the complicated world of relationships and self-worth isn't always easy, but it's incredibly rewarding.

THE BASICS: HOW DOES ATTACHMENT FORM?

Attachment theory is like the "How to Human" guidebook that babies don't come with. John Bowlby and Mary Ainsworth were the dynamic duo who cracked the code on how we bond with others (Ackerman, 2024b). Bowlby's idea was that babies need a strong connection with at least one adult to grow up feeling safe and secure. It's like having a home base in a game of tag—you always know where to run back to when things get scary.

Ainsworth took this idea and ran with it, creating the clever "Strange Situation" test. Imagine it as a reality show for babies—put them in a room, bring in a stranger, have mom leave, then come back. By watching how babies reacted, she identified different attachment styles.

Do you have someone in your life who needs constant reassurance that you still like them? It's like having an inner alarm system that's a bit too sensitive; it goes off at the slightest hint of potential rejection or abandonment.

In romantic relationships, someone with anxious attachment might feel like they're always waiting for their partner to abandon them. They'll send multiple texts when their partner doesn't respond right away, or worry that every little argument means the relationship is doomed. With family, it could look like feeling hurt if parents don't call often enough, struggling to make decisions without family input, or getting overly upset about missing family events. In friendships, you might notice overthinking casual comments from friends, feeling left out if not invited to every gathering, or having trouble believing friends truly care.

Recognizing these patterns is the first step toward changing them. It's like realizing you've been wearing your shoes on the wrong feet—once you know, you can start to make it right. Some practical tips include practicing self-soothing when you feel anxious, communicating openly about your needs instead of hinting or expecting others to read your mind, reminding yourself of times when people have been there for you, and building your self-esteem outside of relationships.

Having an anxious attachment style doesn't make you needy or weak. It just means your inner child is a bit of a worrywart. There are plenty of things you can do to work on your anxiety and grow as a person.

UNDERSTANDING YOUR ATTACHMENT STYLE

If you understand your attachment style, you'll have a better idea of how to interact with others. Imagine you're a little kid learning to swim. Your parent is in the pool with you. Some kids might cling tightly to their parent, afraid to let go. Others might boldly swim away, confident their parent will be there if needed. And some might seem uninterested in their parent's presence altogether. These different approaches to the swimming lesson are a bit like attachment styles in real life.

Why does this matter? Well, our need for connection starts from day one. As babies, we rely completely on our caregivers. This early bond shapes how we view relationships for the rest of our lives. It's like the foundation of a house—it influences everything built on top of it.

Being aware of your attachment style is important because it helps you explore and learn, as feeling secure in your relationships makes you more likely to try new things. It's like having a safe home base. Your attachment style also affects how you relate to others, influencing how you act in friendships and romantic relationships. It determines how you handle emotions, playing a big role in how you deal with stress and strong feelings. It also shapes your happiness and fulfillment, as healthy attachments allow us to experience deep joy and gratitude. Lastly, it influences the closeness of your relationships, affecting how close you allow others to get.

Understanding your attachment style doesn't mean you're stuck with it forever. It's more like recognizing your starting point. Once you're aware of your patterns, you can start to make changes if you need to. There is no "perfect" attachment style. In fact, we can all display characteristics of the different attachment styles. The goal is to develop secure attachments that allow you to feel safe, loved, and capable in your relationships.

CAN YOUR PARENTS' ATTACHMENT STYLE INFLUENCE YOUR OWN ATTACHMENT STYLE?

If your parent was anxious, imagine them as a weather system that's always changing. One day it's sunny and warm; they're super attentive, maybe even clingy. The next day, it's cloudy and cold; they're distant and uninterested. As a kid, you never know what forecast to expect, and this would have been very confusing to you, potentially causing you to become uncertain about what to expect from interactions with them.

So what happens to you? You might become like a little weather detective, always on the lookout for clues about your parent's mood. You're constantly asking yourself, "Do they love me today? Will they be there if I need them?" It's exhausting, right? This can lead to you becoming an anxious person yourself. You might always worry about what others think of you, need lots of reassurance in relationships, feel like people will leave you if you're not perfect, and have a hard time trusting that good things will last.

If your parent was avoidant, picture them as a turtle. When things get tough or too close, they retreat into their shell. You might have found yourself knocking on that shell, trying to get them to come out and connect with you. Growing up like this, you might become either anxious—always trying to get close to people, afraid they'll pull away like your parent did—or avoidant yourself, deciding it's safer to keep your distance so you don't get hurt.

You can learn to build healthier relationships by recognizing these patterns in yourself, communicating your needs clearly, seeking out stable, consistent people, and maybe even talking to a therapist who can help you "rewrite" some of those old patterns.

THE FOUR MAIN ATTACHMENT STYLES

In this section, we're going to explore the four main attachment styles: secure, anxious, avoidant, and disorganized. These terms may sound intimidating, but we're going to break them down in a relatable way. Understanding these styles can help you navigate the tricky terrain of human connections.

THE SECURE ATTACHMENT STYLE

Jake, a 28-year-old software developer, grew up in a loving, supportive family. From an early age, Jake learned that it was okay to express his feelings and that his parents would be there for him when he needed them.

As an adult, Jake's secure attachment style shines through in his relationships. Take his friendship with Mike, for example. When Mike is going through a tough time at work, Jake is there to listen and offer support. He's comfortable being a sounding board, but also knows when to give Mike space to figure things out on his own.

At work, Jake's secure attachment helps him collaborate effectively with his team. He's not afraid to share his ideas or ask for help when he needs it. When his manager gives him constructive criticism, Jake doesn't take it personally. Instead, he sees it as an opportunity to grow and improve his skills.

In his romantic relationship with Amy, Jake's secure attachment is a real strength. They communicate openly about their feelings and needs. When they have disagreements, Jake doesn't worry that Amy will leave him. He trusts in their connection and knows they can work through problems together.

Jake's not perfect, of course. He still has insecurities and bad days like everyone else. But his secure attachment gives him a solid foundation. When life gets tough, he knows how to reach out for support without feeling weak or less masculine.

For Jake, relationships aren't about constant validation or fear of abandonment. They're about genuine connection, mutual support, and the freedom to be himself. His secure attachment style helps him build and maintain healthy, balanced relationships in all areas of his life.

Jake's story shows us what secure attachment looks like in action. It's about feeling safe in your relationships, being able to depend on others while also being independent, and having the emotional tools to handle life's ups and downs (Gupta, 2024). While not everyone starts out with a secure attachment style, understanding it can help us all work toward healthier, more fulfilling connections with the people in our lives.

In adult relationships, a secure attachment style translates to:

- You don't fear being rejected when you share your thoughts and feelings.

- You enjoy time with your partner but also have your own interests and friendships. You don't feel threatened when they do their own thing.

- When conflicts arise, you can discuss issues calmly and work toward solutions together.

- You're there for each other during tough times, offering comfort and understanding.

- You feel worthy of love and capable of giving love in return.

- You see your partner realistically, appreciating their strengths without ignoring their flaws.

- You express your needs clearly and listen actively to your partner's concerns.

Think of secure attachment as having an emotional safety net. It doesn't mean your relationships are perfect or problem-free. Instead, it gives you the confidence to face challenges together, knowing that your bond is strong enough to weather storms.

For those who didn't grow up with secure attachment, the good news is that it can be developed. It takes self-awareness, effort, and often the help of a therapist, but many people learn to build more secure relationships over time.

This might involve:

- recognizing and challenging negative thought patterns

- practicing vulnerability in safe relationships

- learning to set healthy boundaries

- developing better communication skills

- working on self-esteem and self-worth

Secure attachment allows you to enjoy the closeness of relationships without losing yourself in them. It's about finding that place where you can be both connected and independent, creating relationships that enrich your life rather than define it.

THE AVOIDANT ATTACHMENT STYLE

As a therapist, I often see relationships struggling due to mismatched attachment styles. The case of Omar and Leila, a couple in their mid-30s, particularly stands out.

From our first session, I noticed Leila's warm, open demeanor contrasting with Omar's distant, uncomfortable body language. Leila expressed frustration: "I want us to be close, but Omar always pulls away." Omar responded, "I need my space. We don't need to be so dependent on each other."

It was clear—Omar had an avoidant attachment style, while Leila showed a secure attachment style. Let's dive deeper into Omar's avoidant attachment and how it manifested in their relationship:

- Omar feared intimacy and often felt uncomfortable with too much closeness. He'd say things like, "I just need some alone time" or "Why do we need to talk about everything?" This wasn't because he didn't love Leila, but because intimacy felt threatening to his sense of self.

- Omar prided himself on being independent and self-reliant. He'd often say, "I can handle this on my own" or "I don't need help." He rarely shared his feelings or asked for support.

- He found it difficult to express his emotions, which left Leila feeling shut out. When Leila would ask how he felt, Omar would often respond with "I don't know" or "I'm fine."

- When faced with relationship conflicts or stress, Omar's instinct was to withdraw. He'd work late, focus intensely on hobbies, or simply become emotionally distant. This left Leila feeling abandoned when she needed him most.

- Omar found it hard to open up about his fears or insecurities. He'd deflect with humor or change the subject when conversations got too personal.

- He often spoke about the importance of "having your own life" in a relationship. While some independence is healthy, Omar took this to an extreme, keeping parts of his life separate from Leila.

- Although Omar had committed to marriage, he still struggled with deeper emotional commitment. He'd hesitate to make future plans or discuss long-term goals, leaving Leila feeling uncertain.

- Omar rarely expressed his own needs in the relationship. Instead of asking for what he wanted, he'd become resentful or withdrawn.

In our sessions, we worked on addressing these avoidant tendencies:

- helping Omar understand the root of his avoidant behavior and how it impacted his wife

- practicing expressing emotions and needs in a safe environment

- gradually increasing comfort with intimacy through small, manageable steps

- reframing independence and dependence—showing that they can coexist in a healthy relationship

Over time, Omar began to open up more. He started sharing his feelings, even if it was just saying, "I'm not sure how I feel, but I want to figure it out with you." He learned that being close to Leila didn't mean losing himself.

Leila learned to respect Omar's need for space without taking it personally. She'd say, "I understand you need some alone time. I'm here when you're ready to connect."

By recognizing and working with their differences, Omar and Leila built a stronger, more balanced connection. It's not about changing fundamentally, but finding a middle ground where both partners feel secure and respected.

For those who recognize avoidant tendencies in themselves or their partners, remember: Change is possible. With understanding, patience, and often professional help, avoidant individuals can learn to create deeper, more satisfying relationships while maintaining a healthy sense of self.

THE ANXIOUS ATTACHMENT STYLE

Jamal nervously waited for his weekly check-in with his boss, Lisa. Despite two years of positive feedback, these meetings always filled him with dread. When Lisa greeted him with a friendly, "Hi Jamal, how are things going?" he replied anxiously, "Good, I think. Is everything okay? Are you happy with my work?" Lisa looked surprised, assuring him his work was excellent and asking if something was concerning him.

This was Jamal's typical pattern: constantly seeking approval, staying late, and triple-checking everything to prove his worth. It affected all aspects of his work life, even simple interactions with colleagues. Later that day, when his coworker Aisha invited him to lunch, Jamal hesitated, worried about seeming uncommitted if he took a break.

During lunch, Aisha mentioned a workshop she'd attended on attachment styles at work. As she described anxious attachment, Jamal found himself relating to the characteristics:

- Jamal was always on high alert, analyzing every interaction with colleagues and superiors for signs of disapproval or rejection.

- He frequently sought confirmation that his work was satisfactory, often asking for feedback even when it wasn't necessary.

- Despite his good performance, Jamal lived in constant fear of being fired or replaced, interpreting even minor criticisms as threats to his job security.

- When praised, Jamal often doubted the sincerity of the compliment or worried that the person would soon change their mind.

- To prove his worth and prevent potential job loss, Jamal regularly worked long hours and took on extra tasks, often at the expense of his personal life.

- His self-esteem was closely tied to his job performance, making any perceived failure deeply distressing.

- Jamal spent a lot of time analyzing past interactions and worrying about future ones, which often distracted him from his actual work.

- He struggled to "switch off" from work, often checking emails late into the night and worrying about work issues during his personal time.

- Even constructive feedback could send Jamal into a spiral of self-doubt and anxiety.

- He often agreed to take on additional responsibilities or changed his opinions to align with others, fearing disagreement might lead to rejection.

Realizing how much this described his own behavior, Jamal decided it was time to make some changes. He committed to keeping a log of his achievements to remind himself of his capabilities, accepting compliments without immediately doubting them, setting boundaries on his work hours, and considering therapy to work through his insecurities.

DISORGANIZED ATTACHMENT

Zoe's boyfriend, Ryan, surprised her with a visit. At first, Zoe was excited, rushing to hug him. Suddenly, she felt overwhelmed and pushed him away.

"I... I'm sorry," Zoe stammered. "I just remembered I have work to do. Maybe you should go."

Ryan looked confused and hurt. "But I thought we could spend the evening together. Are you okay?"

Zoe's emotions were in turmoil. She wanted Ryan to stay but also felt safer alone. "I don't know," she said. "I want you here, but I also can't handle it. I'm sorry, I'm such a mess."

As Ryan left, Zoe felt both relief and despair. She wanted to run after him but also felt safer alone. This pattern had plagued her relationships for years, and she struggled with disorganized attachment, which is characterized by the following:

- Zoe experienced conflicting desires, for example, craving closeness but fearing it at the same time.

- Her responses were unpredictable, and she reacted warmly one moment and coldly the next.

- She longed for love but is scared of being hurt.

- Zoe struggled to manage her intense emotions and mood swings.

- She struggled to trust others, even loved ones.

- Zoe often felt unworthy or fundamentally flawed.

- Zoe found actual closeness overwhelming.

- Zoe was always on alert for rejection or abandonment.

Childhood trauma or inconsistent caregiving can cause a disorganized attachment style to develop. The contradictory behaviors are attempts to cope with confusing past experiences. The first step to healing is to recognize the patterns.

RELATIONSHIPS BETWEEN THE DIFFERENT ATTACHMENT STYLES

Anxious folks can form relationships with people from any attachment style, and here's how it usually plays out.

ANXIOUS + AVOIDANT

Think of it like a dance where one person always wants to get closer while the other keeps backing away. The anxious partner wants to be close, while the avoidant partner pulls away, as they feel smothered. This creates an exhausting cycle of pursuit and retreat. It's like one person saying, "Hey, let's hang out all the time!" while the other's thinking, *Whoa, I need some space!*

ANXIOUS + SECURE

This is more like a steady waltz. The secure partner can provide the stability and reassurance the anxious partner needs. They're like a calm port in a storm, helping the anxious person feel safe and loved. The secure partner might say, "I'm here for you," and actually mean it, which helps the anxious partner relax and trust more.

ANXIOUS + DISORGANIZED

This relationship can be like a rollercoaster—thrilling but scary. Both partners might swing between wanting closeness and pushing away, creating a lot of confusion. One day they're super close, the next they're distant. It's unpredictable and can leave both feeling unsure about where they stand.

In all these scenarios, open communication and understanding each other's needs are key. It's about learning to say, "Hey, when you do this, I feel that," and working together to find a middle ground that works for both of you.

DISCOVERING YOUR ATTACHMENT STYLE

To begin this process of self-discovery, it's important to ask yourself some key questions and reflect on your past experiences.

Start by analyzing your parents' relationship and the emotional connection between them. The attachment styles of your parents can significantly influence your own. For instance, if one of your parents had an avoidant attachment style, you might have developed either an anxious or avoidant attachment style yourself. Similarly, an anxiously attached parent could lead you to develop anxiety or avoidance in relationships. On the other hand, if you had a securely attached parent, you're more likely to have developed a secure attachment style.

Next, consider your relationship with your parents or other important caregivers during your childhood. These early experiences play a crucial role in shaping your attachment style. Reflect on how your needs were met (or not met) and how that might influence your current approach to relationships.

It's also valuable to look back on your past romantic relationships. What patterns do you notice in your behavior and feelings? Do you tend to worry excessively about being abandoned, or do you find yourself pulling away when things get too close? These patterns can provide important clues about your attachment style.

While there are numerous online tests and psychological questionnaires available to assess attachment styles, it's important to approach these with caution. Choose tests created by specialists and interpret the results carefully. Some reputable options include the Adult Attachment Inventory (AAI) and the Relationship Questionnaire (RQ). You can also find scientifically validated tests on websites like Psychology Today and Psych Central (Crowell et al., 1999). However, the most reliable approach is to undergo a professional psychological assessment.

Finally, ask yourself a fundamental question: In a relationship, do you prefer closeness or distance? This can give you a quick insight into your attachment tendencies. Securely attached people are comfortable with both intimacy and independence. Those with avoidant attachment tend to prioritize distance and independence. Anxious attachment is marked by a strong desire for closeness and frequent worry about the relationship. Disorganized attachment involves a complex mix of desiring yet fearing closeness.

Remember, most people don't fit neatly into one category and may exhibit traits from different attachment styles. The goal of this self-reflection is not to label yourself but to gain a better understanding of your relational patterns. This awareness can be the first step toward developing healthier, more fulfilling relationships, regardless of your starting point.

SEVEN TOXIC PATTERNS YOU NEED TO BREAK

Before embarking on your journey of self-improvement and healing, it's important to be aware of some common pitfalls and patterns to avoid.

1. The anxious-avoidant trap

Sarah and Tom are in a relationship. Sarah constantly worries about their relationship, always seeking reassurance. Tom, on the other hand, feels suffocated and withdraws when Sarah gets too close. This is the anxious-avoidant trap.

In this dynamic, the anxious partner (Sarah) craves intimacy and closeness, while the avoidant partner (Tom) feels overwhelmed and pulls away. This creates a painful cycle where neither person's needs are met. The more Sarah pursues, the more Tom retreats, which makes Sarah even more anxious.

Ideally, you'd want a partner with a secure attachment style who can provide stability. However, if you're currently in an anxious-avoidant relationship, don't despair. Keep reading; you'll find tips to help navigate this situation.

2. Don't rush into relationships

After a breakup, Lisa felt lonely and quickly jumped into a new relationship to fill the void. She ended up repeating old patterns since she hadn't taken time to heal and understand herself.

Always work on yourself first. Take time to understand your needs, reflect on your past experiences, and invest in your personal growth. Entering a relationship when you're still hurting often leads to more pain. Self-reflection and making sense of your childhood experiences are key steps in this process.

3. Avoid partners who send mixed signals

Consider Mark, who's dating someone who's affectionate one day and cold the next. This inconsistent behavior leaves Mark confused and anxious.

Be wary of partners who run hot and cold. If someone is warm and attentive one moment, then distant and unreachable the next, it's a red flag. This kind of behavior can be emotionally draining and prevent you from developing a secure, stable relationship.

4. Stop constantly checking up on your partner

Emma finds herself constantly checking her boyfriend's social media, analyzing his online activity, and feeling anxious when he doesn't respond to texts immediately.

This behavior is harmful to both you and your relationship. Instead of obsessing over your partner's every move, focus on yourself. Read books, pursue hobbies, and get comfortable being alone with your thoughts. This self-focus will help you build confidence and reduce anxiety.

5. Don't shut yourself off

Jack tends to withdraw when he feels vulnerable in relationships. He stops communicating, ignores messages, and retreats into himself.

While it might feel safer to shut down, it's not healthy for your relationships. Try to stay open and communicate, even when it's difficult. It's easier to withdraw, but it's more rewarding to stay engaged.

6. Avoid aggressive reactions

When Kelly feels rejected, she lashes out with anger, trying to provoke a reaction from her partner.

Becoming aggressive or trying to manipulate your partner when you feel insecure will only push them away further. Instead, try to express your feelings calmly and directly.

7. Don't be desperate for attention

Alex constantly seeks validation from his partner, feeling anxious and upset when he doesn't get immediate responses or constant affirmation.

While it's natural to want attention from your partner, there's a fine line between wanting attention and desperately craving it. People with anxious attachment often have wonderful qualities—they're caring, sensitive, and willing to put effort into relationships. However, when the need for attention becomes overwhelming, it can strain the relationship.

Why do you think you crave attention, love, and intimacy so much? This desire often stems from unmet childhood needs or past experiences of rejection or abandonment. Perhaps you learned early on that you had to work hard for love and attention, or that it could be taken away at any moment. Understanding the root of these feelings can help you address them in healthier ways.

REFLECTION WORKSHEET

Think about the seven behaviors described earlier.

Take a moment to reflect on your emotional patterns.

Which behavior are you most vulnerable to?

→ *Why do you think this particular behavior affects you more than the others?*

THE NEXT STEPS

In the upcoming chapters, we'll explore practical strategies to help you develop healthier attachment patterns and more fulfilling relationships.

We'll help you build self-awareness and show you how to identify your emotional triggers, which will in turn help you develop healthy coping mechanisms.

Change doesn't happen overnight but by consistently applying these techniques, you'll gradually shift toward a more secure attachment style and healthier relationships.

Let's turn the page and start this journey of growth and healing together. Are you ready to take the first step?

KEY TAKEAWAYS

- Early childhood experiences shape our attachment styles and affect our adult relationships.

- Attachment styles include: secure, anxious, avoidant, and disorganized.

- The first step toward developing healthier relationship patterns is to understand your own attachment style.

- You should aim to break toxic patterns such as rushing into relationships and constantly seeking reassurance.

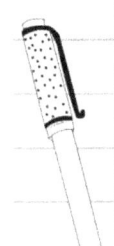

ANXIOUS ATTACHMENT QUIZ

Instructions: Answer each statement honestly, thinking about your close relationships (romantic, friendships, or family).

Use the following scale:

1 - Not at all true for me

2 - Slightly true for me

3 - Somewhat true for me

4 - Fairly true for me

5 - Very true for me

1. I often worry that my partner will leave me, even without clear reasons.

Score: _____

2. I frequently feel insecure in relationships, even when reassured.

Score: _____

3. I have a strong need for closeness and feel uneasy if I don't get the attention I need.

Score: _____

4. I find it hard to trust that others will always be there for me.

Score: _____

5. I overanalyze messages, tone, or behavior, looking for signs that something is wrong.

Score: _____

6. I often feel responsible for other people's emotions.

Score: _____

7. I avoid expressing my needs for fear of seeming too dependent or difficult.

Score: _____

8. When someone pulls away, I cling even more.

Score: _____

9. I have difficulty relaxing in relationships - I always feel I must do more.

Score: _____

10. I feel deeply hurt by rejections, even minor or unintentional ones.

Score: _____

SCORING

Add the scores for each answer. Total score range: 10 to 50.

10-19 points:

You likely have a secure attachment style. You manage closeness and distance in a balanced way.

20-29 points:

You show moderate traits of anxious attachment. You might be somewhat emotionally overprotective.

30-39 points:

You have clear signs of anxious attachment. Fear of rejection and the need for reassurance likely affect your relationships.

40-50 points:

Anxious attachment strongly influences your life. You may struggle with abandonment fears, self-criticism, and regulating intimacy. Therapy could help explore these patterns.

15 minutes,
for 29 days

Dear reader,

I want you to win.

When you win, I win—because my number one goal is to help you conquer what's in front of you and finally build the deep connection you deserve.

That's why I've put together a powerful set of exercises and tasks for the next 29 days. Each takes just 15 minutes a day but will supercharge your recovery journey like you wouldn't believe.

SCAN THE QR CODE TO GET INSTANT ACCESS FOR FREE

cheers,

Andrei Nedelcu

SCAN THE QR CODE TO GET INSTANT ACCESS FOR FREE

PART 2

UNTANGLING THE KNOTS

STEP 1

HEALING ANXIETY ATTACHMENT BY UNDERSTANDING AND MEETING YOUR NEEDS

As I leaned back in my chair, I found myself deeply contemplating the notes from my recent session with Mari. At 28, she's come to me seeking help for what she describes as "constant relationship anxiety." As I reviewed her history, a clear pattern began to emerge in my mind

Mari's childhood, I realize, was marked by significant unpredictability. Her father, an airline pilot, was frequently absent for extended periods. When he was home, his mood swings created an atmosphere of constant tension. Her mother, overwhelmed and emotionally distant, provided little in the way of comfort or stability.

During our session, I asked Mari to tell me about her current relationship. Her response was incredibly revealing. She described obsessively checking her boyfriend's social media, experiencing panic if he took too long to reply to texts, and constantly seeking reassurance of his feelings. The fear of abandonment in her voice was almost palpable.

As a psychologist, I can clearly identify several unmet childhood needs that have likely contributed to Mari's anxious attachment style:

- The inconsistent presence of her father and her mother's emotional unavailability meant Mari never developed a secure base. This lack of stability in her formative years has clearly impacted her ability to feel secure in adult relationships.

- With parents who were preoccupied with their own issues, Mari's emotional needs were often overlooked. This has left her constantly seeking external validation, a pattern that's causing significant distress in her current relationship.

- The lack of consistent, nurturing relationships in childhood has left Mari with an intense craving for closeness, coupled with a fear of intimacy. It's a challenging paradox that I see often in patients with anxious attachment.

- Having learned to be hypervigilant to others' needs and moods, Mari has struggled to develop a strong sense of self. This lack of autonomy makes it difficult for her to feel secure independently of her relationships.

As I prepare for our next session, I'm keenly aware that addressing these core issues will be crucial in helping Mari develop more secure attachment patterns. It will be a challenging journey, but I believe that with increased awareness and targeted interventions, Mari can learn to form healthier, more stable relationships—both with others and with herself.

I'm already formulating some strategies we can explore together. Perhaps we'll start with mindfulness techniques to help her manage anxiety in the moment, coupled with cognitive restructuring to address some of her core beliefs about relationships. Over time, we'll work on building her sense of self-worth and autonomy.

YOUR EMOTIONAL NEEDS

When our emotional needs aren't met as kids, it can really mess with how we handle relationships as adults. It's like we're working with a faulty blueprint, trying to build something stable on shaky ground.

Imagine your partner mentions they're going out with friends. Suddenly, you're hit with a wave of jealousy and fear. You might find yourself asking a million questions about who they're meeting, when they'll be back, and if you can tag along. This isn't because you're controlling by nature, but because deep down, you're terrified of being left behind. It's as if a part of you is constantly on high alert, watching for signs that you might be abandoned.

This fear can lead to some pretty intense behaviors. You might find yourself constantly checking your phone, waiting for a text or call. When your partner doesn't respond right away, your mind starts racing with worst-case scenarios. Are they ignoring you? Did you do something wrong? Have they found someone better? It's exhausting living on this emotional rollercoaster where your mood can swing from ecstatic to devastated based on how much attention you're getting.

It's not just about your partner's actions. You might find being alone unbearable. You might jump from relationship to relationship or stay in ones that aren't good for you just to avoid being on your own. When you do find someone, you put them on a pedestal. They're perfect in your eyes—until they inevitably show their flaws, and then it feels like your whole world is crashing down.

All of these behaviors come from a place of deep need and fear, not malice. You're not trying to be clingy or demanding; you're desperately trying to get your emotional needs met, needs that have gone unfulfilled for a long time. It's like you're trying to fill a bucket with love and affection, but the bucket has holes in it. No matter how much affection you receive, it never seems to be quite enough.

Living like this is exhausting, both for you and for the people you're in relationships with. You first have to recognize these patterns to be able to overcome them. It's not about becoming a completely different person overnight. You slowly have to learn to meet your own emotional needs and to trust that others can be there for you without you having to cling so tightly. It's a journey, and it takes time, but with self-awareness, patience, and maybe some professional help, it's possible to develop healthier, more secure ways of connecting with others. After all, you're not broken—you're just working with the tools you were given.

REFLECTING ON EMOTIONAL NEEDS

Take a moment to slow down and connect with yourself. This page is here to help you gently explore how you've related to your emotional needs so far—and how others in your life have influenced that relationship.

Prompt

How have you related to your emotional needs up until today? What about the people in your life?

*Take your time. There are no wrong answers—only honest reflections. This is your space to notice, without judgment.

R E F L E C T I O N   W O R K S H E E T
Exploring What You Miss Most

Of the four reasons mentioned above, which one do you miss the most in your life?

Why do you think this particular one stands out to you?

How does its absence impact your emotional world or relationships?

WHY IT'S IMPORTANT TO KNOW YOUR NEEDS

Knowing your own needs is like having a map for your life's journey. Let's break down why it's so important, especially for those of us who struggle with anxious attachment.

MEETING YOUR NEEDS IS THE KEY TO HAPPINESS

If you're always hungry but don't know what food you like, how can you ever feel satisfied? The same goes for your emotional needs. When you know what truly makes you feel loved, secure, and fulfilled, you can actively seek those things out. Maybe you need words of affirmation to feel valued or quality time to feel connected. Once you identify these needs, you can work on meeting them yourself and communicating them to others. It's like finally finding the right key to unlock your happiness.

YOU WILL BE TRULY GRATEFUL

When you're clear about your needs, you start to notice when they're being met. It's like suddenly having a new pair of glasses—you see all the good stuff more clearly. That friend who always listens without judgment? You'll appreciate them more. The partner who respects your need for alone time? You'll feel genuinely thankful. This gratitude not only makes you happier but also strengthens your relationships.

YOU WILL UNDERSTAND WHO YOU REALLY ARE

Knowing your needs is like having a heart-to-heart with yourself. As you figure out what makes you tick, you'll start to understand your values, your boundaries, and what really matters to you. Maybe you'll realize that you need creative expression to feel alive or that having a sense of purpose is crucial for your well-being. This self-knowledge is empowering. It helps you make decisions that align with who you truly are rather than who you think you should be.

YOU WILL BE ABLE TO COMMUNICATE THEM LATER

If you can't name your needs, how can you ever ask for them to be met? Once you've done the work to identify what you need, you'll be better equipped to express those needs to others. Instead of feeling frustrated and not knowing why, you can say, "I need some reassurance right now" or "I need some space to recharge." This clear communication is the foundation of healthy relationships.

For those of us with anxious attachment, this process can be challenging. We're often so focused on others' needs that we lose sight of our own. We might worry that having needs makes us needy or that expressing them will push people away. The truth is that understanding and communicating your needs is a sign of emotional maturity and self-respect.

Start small. Pay attention to when you feel content, anxious, or frustrated. What is happening in those moments? What do you wish was different? These are clues to your needs. Write them down and reflect on them. It's okay if it takes time—you are learning a new language, the language of your own heart.

Knowing your needs doesn't mean you expect others to meet all of them all the time. It's about understanding yourself better so you can take care of yourself and communicate clearly with others.

UNDERSTANDING YOUR EMOTIONAL NEEDS

Sometimes, we don't even know what we need until something happens that makes us upset.

Let's look at an example to understand this better:

Susan got really angry with Jack after he told her about meeting up with Emily, his childhood best friend. They had stayed close over the years.

Now, you might wonder: *Why was Susan so upset? What was really going on inside her?*

- Maybe Susan felt left out or not important enough.

- She might have worried that Jack liked Emily more than her.

- Old memories of being left behind by friends or family could have come back.

What Susan really needed at that moment was to feel safe and secure in her relationship with Jack.

DIGGING DEEPER: WHAT'S BEHIND YOUR FEELINGS?

Often, when we react strongly to something, there is a deeper need that is not being met. In Susan's case, her anger was probably covering up a fear of being abandoned.

So, instead of just being angry, Susan could try to understand herself better. She could ask herself:

- What am I really feeling right now?

- What do I need to feel better?

- Why is this situation bothering me so much?

IDENTIFYING YOUR NEEDS

When you are upset, try asking yourself what you really need. Is it love, acceptance, support, respect, trust, and so on?

It can help to write these feelings down in a journal. This way, you can start to see patterns in what you need.

CREATING YOUR NEEDS HIERARCHY

Just like some things are more important than others in life, some emotional needs are more important to us than others. You can make a list of your needs, putting the most important ones at the top. This is called a "hierarchy of needs."

For example:

- feeling safe and secure (most important)

- being loved and accepted

- feeling respected

- having support

- feeling encouraged (less crucial, but still nice)

Your list might look different, and that's okay. Everyone's needs are a bit different (David, 2022).

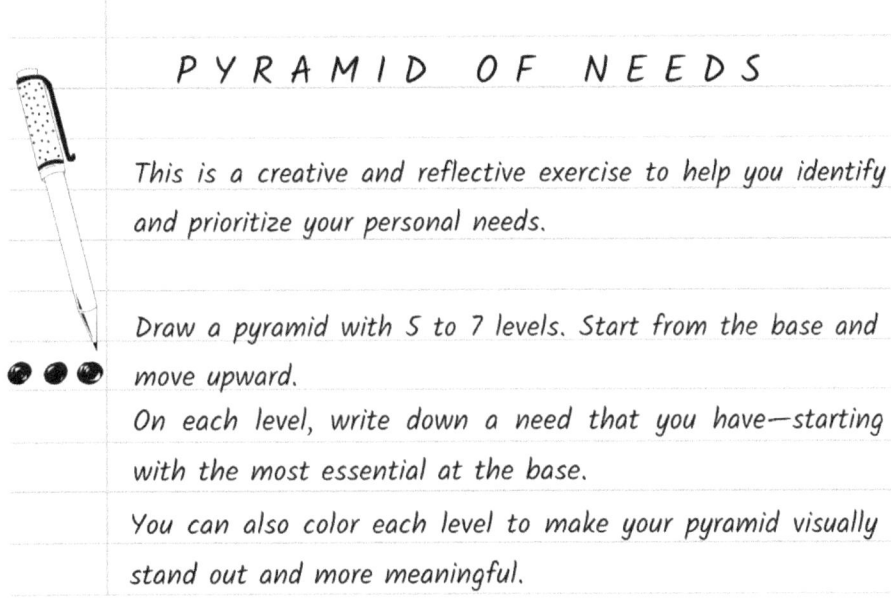

PYRAMID OF NEEDS

This is a creative and reflective exercise to help you identify and prioritize your personal needs.

Draw a pyramid with 5 to 7 levels. Start from the base and move upward.

On each level, write down a need that you have—starting with the most essential at the base.

You can also color each level to make your pyramid visually stand out and more meaningful.

Use the space below to draw your pyramid:

Reflection (Optional)

What did you notice while thinking about your needs?

USING YOUR NEEDS HIERARCHY

Once you know what your most important needs are, you can:

- Communicate better: Tell others what you need instead of just getting upset.

- Make better choices: Do things that meet your most important needs.

- Understand yourself: Know why you react the way you do in different situations.

Understanding your needs doesn't mean you always get what you want, but it does help you handle tough situations better and have healthier relationships.

REFLECTING ON UNMET NEEDS

Sometimes, when we're upset or struggling, it's not just about what's happening right now. Our past experiences, especially times when our needs weren't met, can affect how we feel and react today.

UNDERSTANDING THE PATTERN

Imagine you have a sore tooth. You might take painkillers to feel better, but that doesn't fix the real problem. The same goes for our emotions. We might try to deal with our feelings in the moment, but the real cause might be something from our past.

For example, if you often feel anxious when your partner goes out with friends, it might not just be about trust in your current relationship. It could be connected to times in your childhood when you felt left out or abandoned.

EXPLORING YOUR PAST NEEDS

To understand yourself better, try asking:

- What needs did I have as a child that weren't met?

- Were there times I felt unloved, unsafe, or unimportant?

- What did I wish for but never got?

This isn't about blaming anyone. It's about understanding yourself better so you can heal and grow.

WRITING A LETTER TO YOURSELF

Writing a letter to yourself can be a powerful way to explore your unmet needs. Here is an example:

Dear [Your Name],

I'm writing this letter to you with kindness and understanding. I want to talk about some of the needs you have had for a long time but have not been able to fulfill.

When you were little, I know you really wanted to feel safe and protected. Remember how scared you felt when Mom and Dad argued? You needed someone to hold you and tell you everything would be okay. I'm sorry you didn't get that then.

As you grew up, you longed to feel truly seen and understood. In school, you tried so hard to fit in but often felt like an outsider. You needed friends who accepted you for who you are, not who they wanted you to be. That must have been really hard.

I know you have always yearned for unconditional love—the kind where you don't have to be perfect to be worthy. Maybe that's why you try so hard in your relationships now. You are still looking for that complete acceptance you missed out on before.

You have also needed the freedom to express your true feelings. Growing up, you often had to be the "strong one" or the "happy one." It's okay to admit that sometimes you just wanted to cry or be angry without feeling guilty about it.

Lastly, you have needed to feel capable and confident. Those times when you were criticized or compared to others really hurt. You needed encouragement and support to believe in yourself.

It's okay that these needs weren't met before. It wasn't your fault. Now that you understand them, you can start to take care of yourself in the ways you have always needed.

You are strong, you are worthy, and you are doing your best. I am proud of you for looking inside yourself like this. It is not easy, but it is so important.

With love and compassion, [Your Name]

MOVING FORWARD

Now that you've identified some of your unmet needs, you can

- be gentle with yourself when these old feelings come up.

- look for healthy ways to meet these needs now.

- communicate your needs clearly in your current relationships.

- seek support from friends, family, or a therapist if you need help healing.

Remember, understanding your past needs doesn't mean you're stuck there. It's a step toward taking better care of yourself now and in the future.

KEY TAKEAWAYS

- Childhood experiences with inconsistent or emotionally unavailable parents can lead to relationship anxiety in adulthood.

- It emphasizes the importance of understanding one's emotional needs, especially for those with anxious attachment.

- It is crucial to know your own needs, including the benefits of increased happiness, gratitude, self-understanding, and improved communication in relationships.

CHOOSE A THOUGHT AND PRACTICE

This space is for you to slow down, focus on one recurring thought, and gently explore it.

 The Thought You Chose:

- When does this thought usually show up?

- What does this thought make you feel?

- What would you tell a friend who had this thought?

- How could you reframe this thought with more compassion?

Remember! Thoughts are not facts. You are allowed to pause, reflect, and rewrite your story.

STEP 2

HEALING ANXIOUS ATTACHMENT BY MASTERING YOUR THINKING

I like to tell you about Cassie, a 28-year-old woman I've been working with. Cassie is great at her job as a graphic designer, but she often gets tangled up in worried thoughts. Let me walk you through a day in Cassie's life to show you how anxious thinking works.

Cassie's day started when she checked her email and saw a message from her boss asking to meet that afternoon. Right away, Cassie's mind went into worry mode. *Oh no*, she thought, *I must be in trouble. Maybe they're going to fire me!* Cassie's heart started racing, and she felt sick to her stomach. She couldn't focus on her work all morning because she was so worried.

Now, this is something I see a lot. Cassie jumped to the worst possible conclusion without any real evidence. We call this "fortune telling"—trying to predict the future and always predicting it'll be bad. It's a common trick our anxious minds play on us.

When Cassie finally went to the meeting, her boss actually wanted to give her a bigger role in a new project. All that worry was for nothing. This happens a lot with anxiety; we often fear the worst, but the worst rarely happens.

Later that day, Cassie got invited to a party. Instead of feeling excited, she started worrying again. *What if I don't know anyone? People will think I'm boring.* These thoughts made Cassie decide to stay home.

This is another thing I often see—anxious thoughts making people avoid situations that might actually be fun. By staying home, Cassie felt relief in the short term, but she missed out on a chance to have a good time and maybe prove to herself that parties aren't so scary after all.

So, how am I helping Cassie? Well, we're working on a few things:

- Spotting worry thoughts. I'm teaching Cassie to notice when she's having anxious thoughts. Just realizing "Oh, this is my anxiety talking" can be really powerful.

- Questioning those thoughts. We practice asking, "Is this thought really true? What evidence do I have?" Often, we realize our anxious thoughts aren't based on facts.

- Trying out new things. Little by little, we're encouraging Cassie to do things that make her anxious, like going to a party for just 30 minutes. This helps her see that she can handle more than she thinks.

- We're learning some simple breathing exercises to help Cassie feel calmer in her body when she's stressed.

- We're practicing mindfulness and paying attention to the present moment instead of worrying about the future.

Cassie's story probably sounds familiar to a lot of people. Many of us struggle with anxious thoughts from time to time. The good news is, with some practice, we can get better at managing these thoughts.

WHY ARE THOUGHTS SO IMPORTANT?

Our thoughts are like the glasses we wear to see the world. They shape everything we experience. Let's explore why our thoughts are so powerful and how they affect us.

1. THOUGHTS CREATE OUR VIEW OF THE WORLD

Imagine two people looking at the same cloudy sky. One thinks, *What a gloomy day!* while the other thinks, *The plants will love this rain!* Same sky, different thoughts, totally different experiences.

Our thoughts color everything we see and experience. They're like filters that can make the world seem bright and full of opportunities or dark and full of problems.

2. THOUGHTS MAKE US FEEL WHAT WE FEEL

Our feelings don't just appear out of nowhere. They come from our thoughts. For example:

- If you think, *I'm going to fail this test*, you'll probably feel anxious and worried.

- If you think, *I've studied hard and I'll do my best*, you might feel calm and confident.

Remember Susan from our earlier example? When she thought Jack might leave her for his friend, she felt angry and scared. Her thoughts about the situation created those feelings.

3. THOUGHTS CAN TORTURE US OR HELP US

Our minds can be our best friends or our worst enemies. Negative thoughts can keep us up at night, make us doubt ourselves, and hold us back from trying new things.

Positive, encouraging thoughts can give us the courage to face challenges, help us feel good about ourselves, and push us to achieve our goals.

4. THOUGHTS DETERMINE WHAT WE DO NEXT

Our actions often follow our thoughts. For instance:

- If you think, *I'm too tired to exercise*, you'll probably stay on the couch.

- If you think, *A quick walk will give me more energy*, you're more likely to get up and move.

Our thoughts can motivate us to take action or convince us to give up before we even try.

5. THOUGHTS HELP IDENTIFY OUR NEEDS

Here's an important point: Your thoughts about a situation can help you figure out what you really need. Let's break this down:

- Notice your thought: *I'm worried Jack will leave me for his friend.*

- Identify the feeling: Anxiety, fear.

- Dig deeper: What does this thought tell you about your needs?

- Uncover the need: In this case, the need might be for security in your relationship.

By paying attention to your thoughts, you can uncover your deeper needs.

PUTTING IT INTO PRACTICE

Now that you know how important thoughts are, what can you do?

- Pay attention to your thoughts. Notice what you're telling yourself throughout the day.

- Question your thoughts. Are they true? Are they helpful?

- Try to replace unhelpful thoughts with more balanced ones. Instead of *I'm going to mess this up*, try *I'll do my best and learn from this experience.*

- Use your thoughts to understand your needs. When you have a strong reaction to something, look at your thoughts to figure out what need is behind them.

Changing how you think takes practice, and over time, you can learn to use your thoughts to create a more positive experience of the world and understand yourself better.

IDENTIFYING THOUGHTS RELATED TO ANXIOUS ATTACHMENT

When you're feeling insecure in a relationship, worrying thoughts could pop up. Those are the ones that make your stomach do flip-flops and your mind race. They are often signs of anxious attachment, and they can be really tough to deal with.

You're at a party with your partner, and you notice them laughing and chatting with someone else across the room. Suddenly, your brain goes into overdrive. You might find yourself thinking:

Why is she spending so much time talking to that person? Am I boring compared to them? What if she realizes she'd rather be with someone else? Maybe I'm not attractive enough to keep her interested. She looks happier with them than she does with me. I bet she's thinking about how she can politely end our relationship. I need to go over there right now. I can't bear seeing her enjoy someone else's company.

These thoughts start racing through your mind, even though your partner is just having a normal conversation at a social event. Your heart rate increases, your palms get sweaty, and you feel an overwhelming urge to intervene or leave the party altogether.

This scenario shows how anxious attachment can manifest in social situations, causing you to misinterpret normal interactions and feel threatened by your partner's independence. These thoughts aren't a reality but rather a reflection of your own insecurities and fears. It's like our brain is trying to protect us by imagining the worst, but it often does more harm than good.

So, what can you do about it? First, try to recognize these thoughts when they pop up. Challenge them by asking the following:

- Is there any real evidence for this thought?

- What would I tell a friend if they were having this thought?

- Is there another way to look at this situation?

It can also help to talk to someone you trust about these feelings. Sometimes, just saying them out loud can make them less scary.

HOW TO START WORKING WITH YOUR THOUGHTS

Imagine your thoughts are like a messy room. Sometimes it's hard to find what you need because everything's all over the place. Working with your thoughts is like tidying up that room.

First, find a special place for your thoughts. It could be a notebook you keep on your nightstand or a notes app on your phone. This is your thought journal.

Now, ask yourself: "What goes through my mind when I'm feeling anxious about my relationship?" Write these thoughts down. You might call this list "My Worry Thoughts" or "My Relationship Fears."

Think about where these thoughts come from. Maybe you had a bad experience in the past, or you saw your parents struggle in their relationship. Understanding the root of your thoughts can help you see them more clearly.

As you write, you'll start to notice patterns. Some thoughts might pop up more often than others. Some might hurt more than others. Pay attention to when and where you have these thoughts. Do they come up when you're alone? When your partner is busy?

The tricky part is figuring out which thoughts are true and which ones aren't. It's like being a detective in your own mind. Look for evidence. If you think, *My partner doesn't care about me*, ask yourself: Is that really true? What are some times when they've shown they do care?

It can be really helpful to talk to people you trust about these thoughts. They might see things you don't, like a friend spotting something you missed in that messy room.

Remember, you don't have to tackle all your thoughts at once. Pick one thought to work on, like *I'm not good enough*. Focus on challenging and changing that one thought.

How might different people think in your situation? How would your best friend see things? Your grandma? A relationship expert? This can help you find new ways of looking at your situation.

Here's a fun exercise: Act as if your anxious thoughts are wrong. If you usually think, *He's going to leave me*," try acting as if you believe, *He's committed to our relationship*. See how this changes your behavior and feelings.

When those anxious thoughts come back (and they probably will), ask yourself, "How would I like to think about this instead?" This helps you start replacing negative thoughts with more positive, realistic ones.

Remember, everyone's mind works differently. What helps one person might not work for another. The key is to keep trying different approaches until you find what works for you.

By understanding your thoughts better, you're not just tidying up your mental space. You're also learning more about yourself, what you need in relationships, and how to communicate better with your partner. It's like creating a road map for

KEY TAKEAWAYS

- Thoughts shape our perception of the world, influencing our emotions and determining our actions. Negative thought patterns can reinforce anxiety and insecurity in relationships.

- Strategies for identifying and working with anxious thoughts include journaling, questioning the validity of thoughts, and trying to view situations from different perspectives.

IDENTIFYING THOUGHTS RELATED TO ANXIOUS ATTACHMENT

Purpose: Learn to recognize anxious thoughts and reframe them into more realistic perspectives.

STEP 1: Notice the Situation

Describe a recent moment when you felt insecure in a relationship.

→ Example: I was at a party and my partner was talking to someone else.

My situation:

STEP 2: Write Down Your Automatic Thoughts

List the thoughts that ran through your mind during that moment.

→ Example: Maybe they'd rather be with that person.

My thoughts:

STEP 3: Examine the Thought

Pick one thought and answer the questions below honestly:

→ Is there any real evidence for this thought?

→ What would I tell a friend who had this thought?

→ Is there another, more balanced way to see the situation?

STEP 4: Reframe the Thought

Rewrite the thought in a more realistic and compassionate way.

Example: My partner is just being friendly. That doesn't mean they don't care about me.

→ My new perspective:

STEP 5: Express Your Feelings

Who is someone you trust that you could talk to about this?

Name / relationship:

What could you say?

Helpful Reminders!

- Thoughts are not facts.
- Insecurity can speak loudly, but it doesn't always speak the truth.
- Becoming aware of these patterns is the first step toward healing.

STEP 3

HEALING ANXIETY ATTACHMENT BY MANAGING YOUR TRIGGERS WITH SELF-REGULATING

I once worked with a client named Aisha. She was a bright, ambitious 28-year-old who struggled with impulsive spending. Aisha would often buy things she didn't need, maxing out her credit cards on clothing, gadgets, and home décor. This behavior was causing her significant stress and financial problems.

Aisha's case clearly showed why self-regulation is so crucial. She knew her spending was out of control, but she couldn't seem to stop herself in the moment. When she saw something she liked, she'd buy it without thinking about the consequences.

We worked together to develop her self-regulation skills. First, we identified her spending triggers—boredom, stress, and the temporary high she got from buying something new. Then, we practiced techniques to pause and think before making a purchase.

Aisha learned to ask herself questions like: "Do I really need this?" and "How will I feel about this purchase tomorrow?" She also started leaving her credit cards at home and giving herself a 24-hour "cooling off" period before big purchases.

Over time, Aisha got better at controlling her impulses. She still enjoyed shopping, but she did it mindfully and within her budget. Her stress levels dropped, and she started saving money for the first time in years.

This case shows how self-regulation can make a huge difference in someone's life. By learning to pause, think, and make conscious choices, Aisha gained control over her behavior and improved her well-being. It's a skill that helps in all areas of life, from managing emotions to achieving long-term goals.

EMOTIONAL REGULATION REFLECTION

Take a few moments to reflect on moments when your emotions feel the most intense or difficult to manage.
Be honest with yourself—this isn't about judgment, but about self-awareness.

→ Write down below all the important situations in which you usually struggle to regulate your emotions:

WHAT IS SELF-REGULATION?

Being able to self-regulate means you can manage your thoughts, emotions, and behaviors in ways that help you achieve your goals. It's like having an internal control system that helps you navigate life's ups and downs. When you self-regulate, you're able to calm yourself down when you're upset, motivate yourself when you're feeling lazy, and focus your attention on what's important. It's not about suppressing your feelings, but rather about understanding and managing them effectively.

Think of self-regulation as your inner coach. This coach helps you make good decisions, even when you're faced with temptations or challenges. It's the voice that reminds you to take a deep breath when you're angry or to keep working on a task even when you feel like giving up. Self-regulation allows you to respond thoughtfully to situations instead of reacting impulsively.

WHY IS IT IMPORTANT FOR THOSE WITH ANXIOUS ATTACHMENT TO BE ABLE TO CALM DOWN?

For people with anxious attachment, learning to self-regulate is particularly crucial. Those with anxious attachment often struggle with intense emotions and fears about their relationships, which can lead to stress and relationship difficulties. By developing strong self-regulation skills, they can gain more control over these challenging emotions and behaviors.

Firstly, self-regulation reduces stress and anxiety. When you can calm yourself down, it's like having a built-in stress reliever. For example, if you're anxiously waiting for a text back from your partner, instead of letting your mind race with worst-case scenarios, you can use self-regulation techniques like deep breathing or positive self-talk to keep yourself grounded. This ability to soothe yourself can significantly reduce overall anxiety levels.

Secondly, self-regulation improves relationships. It helps you respond to situations rather than react impulsively. Let's say your partner is late for a date. Instead of immediately assuming they don't care and sending a flurry of upset messages, you can pause, take a breath, and consider other possibilities. This measured approach leads to fewer conflicts and misunderstandings, creating a more stable and positive relationship environment.

Lastly, self-regulation promotes better decision-making. When you're calm and collected, you're more likely to make choices that align with your long-term goals and values. Think of it like shopping for groceries. If you go to the store hungry (emotionally dysregulated), you might impulse-buy a bunch of junk food. But if you eat a snack first (self-regulate), you're more likely to stick to your healthy shopping list. The same principle applies to relationship decisions—when you're regulated, you're more likely to act in ways that support healthy, secure attachments.

EMOTIONAL SELF-REGULATION: WHY IT MATTERS

Practicing emotional self-regulation doesn't just help you feel better in the moment—it shapes your whole life. Take a moment to reflect on what emotional self-regulation can do for you. Below, write down five personal benefits you believe it brings to your life. Be specific, and make it meaningful.

Write down clearly and specifically 5 major personal benefits of emotional self-regulation:

1.

2.

3.

4.

5.

THE CONNECTION BETWEEN ATTACHMENT, EMOTIONS, AND THOUGHTS

EARLY ATTACHMENT AND ADULT EMOTIONS

Imagine your childhood experiences as the foundation of a house. If that foundation is strong and secure, the house (your adult self) is more likely to weather storms well. For example, if you grew up with parents who were consistently there for you, you might find it easier to trust others and manage your emotions as an adult.

If your early experiences were less stable—maybe your caregivers were inconsistent or unavailable—it's like building a house on shaky ground. As an adult, you might struggle more with trust or emotional regulation. For example, you might find yourself getting anxious easily in relationships or having trouble expressing your feelings.

EMOTIONAL CYCLES IN ANXIOUS ATTACHMENT

For people with anxious attachment, emotions can feel like a roller coaster. Here's a typical cycle:

ANTICIPATORY ANXIETY

Imagine you're waiting for a text from your partner. Instead of just waiting, your mind starts racing: *Why haven't they texted? Are they mad at me? Did I do something wrong?*

FEAR OF ABANDONMENT

This anxiety might spiral into deeper fears. *What if they're going to break up with me? I can't handle being alone!*

SEEKING REASSURANCE

To calm these fears, you might find yourself constantly reaching out. You might text repeatedly, ask for more affection, or need frequent verbal confirmations of love.

TEMPORARY RELIEF

When you get that reassurance, you feel better... for a while. But soon, the cycle starts again.

THE INTERPLAY OF THOUGHTS, EMOTIONS, AND BEHAVIORS

Think of your mind as a busy intersection where thoughts, feelings, and actions are constantly crossing paths and influencing each other. Here's how it works:

- The context triggers thoughts. Let's say you're at a party where you don't know anyone. This situation might trigger thoughts like, *I don't fit in here. People will think I'm boring.*

- Thoughts influence your feelings and behaviors. These thoughts might make you feel anxious and lead you to stand in the corner, avoiding conversation.

- Feelings and behaviors create new thoughts. As you stand there alone, you might think, *See? I knew I didn't belong here. I'm so awkward.*

The good news is that because these elements are so interconnected, changing one can influence the others. For example:

CHANGING BEHAVIOR TO INFLUENCE THOUGHTS

If you push yourself to talk to one person at the party, you might realize, *Hey, that wasn't so bad. Maybe I can do this after all.*

CHANGING EMOTIONS TO INFLUENCE THOUGHTS

If you use deep breathing to calm your anxiety before the party, you might approach the situation with more positive thoughts.

CHANGING THOUGHTS TO INFLUENCE EMOTIONS AND BEHAVIORS

If you challenge your negative thoughts (*just because I'm nervous doesn't mean I'm boring*), you might feel more confident and be more likely to engage with others.

Understanding this connection gives you more control over your experiences. It's like having access to multiple levers—you can pull on thoughts, emotions, or behaviors to create positive changes in your life. This is particularly powerful for those with anxious attachment, as it provides multiple entry points for breaking negative cycles and building more secure, satisfying relationships.

WHAT TRIGGERS YOU?

Understanding your triggers can help you manage anxious attachment. Triggers are like emotional alarm bells—specific situations, behaviors, or events that set off strong emotional reactions in you, often tied to past experiences or fears. For someone with anxious attachment, these triggers often relate to fears of abandonment or rejection.

Knowing your triggers is like having a map of emotional landmines. When you know where these "mines" are, you can either avoid them or prepare yourself to handle them better. You'll have more control over your reactions and will be able to react calmly.

To identify your triggers, pay attention to when you feel sudden spikes of anxiety or insecurity in your relationship. Ask yourself: What just happened? What was I thinking about? What does this remind me of from my past? Keep a journal or notes on your phone to track these moments. Over time, you'll start to see patterns.

Once you know your personal triggers, you can communicate them calmly to your partner, developing coping strategies for when you're triggered, challenging the thoughts that come up, and gradually building more secure attachment patterns.

AUTOGENIC TRAINING

Autogenic training is a powerful relaxation technique that empowers individuals to achieve a state of deep calm and reduce stress through self-suggestion. Developed in the 1930s by German psychiatrist Johannes Schultz, this method has gained recognition for its effectiveness in promoting both physical and mental well-being (Lindberg, 2019).

Autogenic training uses focused attention and specific verbal phrases to induce relaxation. You learn to direct your awareness to different body parts, cultivating sensations of heaviness and warmth. Your parasympathetic nervous system will be activated, which counteracts the effects of stress and promotes a calm state.

A typical autogenic training session progresses through several stages, each focusing on a different aspect of bodily awareness:

- heaviness in the limbs

- warmth in the limbs

- cardiac regulation

- breathing regulation

- abdominal warmth

- cooling of the forehead

Let's take a more detailed look at how you can do these exercises (*Autogenic Training*, n.d.).

GETTING STARTED

First, you need to set the scene. You'll need to find a quiet place where you can be undisturbed for about 20 minutes. Dim the lights if you can. The goal is to create a calm environment.

Then you need to find the position that will work for you. If you use the armchair method, you can sit with your back straight but not stiff. Rest your head against the backrest. Place your feet flat on the floor, about shoulder-width apart. Let your arms rest comfortably on the armrests or in your lap.

Should you choose the lying down method, lie on your back on a bed or yoga mat. You can put a small pillow under your head if it's more comfortable. Let your arms rest at your sides, palms facing up.

THE WEEKLY PROGRESSION

WEEK 1: THE BASICS

1. Start with the mantra: "I am calm, relaxed" (repeat 12–16 times).

2. Move to the weight exercise (details below).

3. End with "I am calm, relaxed" (12–16 times).

WEEK 2: ADDING WARMTH

1. Start with the mantra: "I am calm, relaxed" (repeat 12–16 times).

2. Move to the weight exercise (details below).

3. Add the heat exercise (details below).

4. End with "I am calm, relaxed" (12–16 times).

WEEK 3: HEART AND BREATHING

1. Start with the mantra: "I am calm, relaxed" (repeat 12–16 times).

2. Move to the weight exercise (details below).

3. Add the heat exercise (details below).

4. Add "The heart beats calmly and rhythmically. Breathing is regular" (12–16 times).

5. End with "I am calm, relaxed" (12–16 times).

WEEK 4: SOLAR PLEXUS

1. Start with the mantra: "I am calm, relaxed" (repeat 12–16 times).

2. Move to the weight exercise (details below).

3. Add the heat exercise (details below).

4. Add "The heart beats calmly and rhythmically. Breathing is regular" (12–16 times).

5. Include "The solar plexus is warm." (12–16 times)

6. End with "I am calm, relaxed" (12–16 times).

WEEK 5: COOL FOREHEAD

1. Start with the mantra: "I am calm, relaxed" (repeat 12–16 times).

2. Move to the weight exercise (details below).

3. Add the heat exercise (details below).

4. Add "The heart beats calmly and rhythmically. Breathing is regular" (12–16 times).

5. Include "The solar plexus is warm" (12–16 times).

6. Add "The forehead is cool" (12–16 times).

7. End with "I am calm, relaxed" (12–16 times).

WEEK 6: PERSONAL MANTRA

1. Start with the mantra: "I am calm, relaxed" (repeat 12–16 times).

2. Move to the weight exercise (details below).

3. Add the heat exercise (details below).

4. Add "The heart beats calmly and rhythmically. Breathing is regular" (12–16 times).

5. Include "The solar plexus is warm" (12–16 times).

6. Add "The forehead is cool" (12–16 times).

7. Create and add your personal positive affirmation (12–16 times).

8. End with "I am calm, relaxed" (12–16 times).

DETAILED EXERCISES

Weight exercise: Imagine a pleasant heaviness spreading through your body. Go through each part:

- "My right arm is heavy" (12–16 times).

- "My left arm is heavy" (12–16 times).

- "Both arms are heavy" (12–16 times).

- "My right leg is heavy" (12–16 times).

- "My left leg is heavy" (12–16 times).

- "Both legs are heavy" (12–16 times).

- "My arms and legs are heavy" (12–16 times).

- "My whole body is heavy" (12–16 times).

Heat exercise: Similar to the weight exercise, but focus on warmth:

- "My right arm is warm" (and so on, following the same pattern as the weight exercise)

Heart and breathing: Combine with your natural breath. As you inhale, think *The heart beats calmly*, and as you exhale, think *and rhythmically*. Then *breathing is regular* with the next breath cycle.

Solar plexus: Imagine a warm, glowing sun in the center of your chest as you repeat the phrase.

Cool forehead: Envision a cool, refreshing sensation across your forehead.

Personal mantra: Choose something meaningful to you, like "I am confident and capable" or "I face challenges with ease."

Tips for success:

- Consistency is vital. Try to practice at the same time each day. Many find mornings or evenings work best.

- It might feel weird or ineffective at first. Just be patient. Your body is learning a new skill.

- Focus on sensations. Don't worry if you are doing it correctly. Instead, pay attention to how your body feels.

- As you get more practiced, you might find you need fewer repetitions to feel the effects.

- Once you're comfortable with the technique, try using parts of it in stressful situations. Even a few deep breaths and "I am calm, relaxed" can help.

- If you miss a day, don't stress. Just pick up where you left off.

- Keep a journal of how you feel before and after each session.

If you practice regularly, your ability to enter a relaxed state quickly and efficiently will improve. This skill can help you manage stress-related conditions and improve your overall quality of life. Research has shown that autogenic training may help address a variety of health concerns, including:

- anxiety disorders

- mild to moderate depression

- insomnia and sleep disturbances

- hypertension

- tension headaches and migraines

- asthma and other respiratory conditions (Arlin, 2023)

To enjoy the most benefit from autogenic training, you should practice regularly, ideally two to three times daily. Sessions typically last for 3 to 15 minutes, though longer sessions may be beneficial as you become more proficient. Autogenic training is perfectly safe; however, people with mental health conditions should first speak to a doctor before starting this practice.

Autogenic training isn't just for special occasions; you can use it anytime, anywhere. It's like having a stress-relief button in your pocket. Need a quick breather at work? Feeling nervous before a big meeting? Can't seem to wind down at bedtime? Autogenic training can help you out. With a little practice, you can use it to find your calm center, even when life gets hectic.

This is why it's so important to practice and master these exercises beforehand; otherwise, you won't be able to use them effectively during moments of need. You need to be able to use them in a way that they become part of your automatic responses when under pressure.

To wrap it up, autogenic training is a solid, science-backed way to relax and dial down stress. It's all about using the connection between your mind and body to feel better. In today's world, where stress seems to be lurking around every corner, having a way to calm yourself down is super important. Autogenic training shows us just how powerful our minds can be; with some focused attention and a few simple phrases, we can change how we feel both mentally and physically.

WHAT SHOULD I DO WHEN I'M FEELING DOWN?

There are several practical things you can do to improve when you're feeling down.

MINDFULNESS

Mindfulness is about being present in the moment without judgment. It's like hitting the pause button on your worries. Try the 5-4-3-2-1 technique: Look around and name 5 things you can see, 4 things you can touch, 3 things you can hear, 2 things you can smell, and 1 thing you can taste. This helps ground you in the present and can calm a racing mind.

DEEP BREATHING

This method can quickly reduce stress and anxiety. Box breathing is a simple but effective exercise. Breathe in for 4 counts, hold for 4 counts, breathe out for 4 counts, and hold for 4 counts. Imagine tracing a box as you do this. Repeat for a few minutes and feel the calm wash over you.

EXERCISE

Exercise is like a natural mood booster, and it doesn't have to be complicated or intense. When you're feeling down, why not try a dance break? Find your favorite upbeat song and dance like you're alone at a concert or like you're in a cheesy '80s movie montage. Swing your arms, shake your hips, and jump around.

Nature has a way of soothing our souls and putting our problems in perspective. Take a mindful walk outside. Notice the trees, the sky, the birds. Feel the ground under your feet. Breathe in the fresh air. Even a brief connection with nature can be refreshing and uplifting.

As you move, your body starts releasing endorphins, those feel-good chemicals that act like natural painkillers and mood elevators. It's like your body's own little pharmacy.

GRATITUDE JOURNAL

Writing down your thoughts can help you process emotions and gain perspective. A gratitude journal can be particularly powerful. Write down three things you're grateful for, no matter how small. Maybe it's the warm sun on your face or your delicious cup of coffee. Focusing on the positives can shift your mood in surprising ways.

GUIDED MEDITATION

Guided meditation is like having a personal relaxation coach in your ear. Find a comfortable position before trying body scan meditation. Close your eyes and focus on the different sensations in each part of your body without trying to change them. Start with your toes. Gradually work your way up to the top of your head. This can help your body release tension of which you hadn't even been aware.

These techniques aren't about forcing happiness but rather about gently shifting your state of mind. Try different ones to see what works best for you.

MY CLEAR, CONCRETE PLAN FOR WHEN I'M FEELING DOWN

When difficult emotions hit, it's easy to feel lost or overwhelmed. Having a clear plan in place can help you navigate those moments with more intention and self-compassion.

- What are some signs that I'm starting to spiral or feel low?

- What can I tell myself in the moment to pause and ground?

- Who is someone I can reach out to for support?

- What can I say to them?

What are 3 simple things I can do to soothe myself?

(e.g., take a walk, listen to music, journal)

A reminder I want to keep close for when I'm struggling:

KEY TAKEAWAYS

- We look at the importance of self-regulation for people with anxious attachment and highlight how it can reduce stress, improve relationships, and promote better decision-making.

- The relaxation technique of autogenic training is described in detail, including its history, methodology, and potential benefits. It provides a step-by-step guide for practicing this relaxation technique.

- The content offers several practical strategies for managing negative emotions, including mindfulness exercises, deep breathing techniques, physical exercise, journaling, and guided meditation.

PART 3

BUILDING SELF-ESTEEM—THE FOUNDATION FOR A FULFILLED LIFE

STEP 4

REWIRING YOUR BRAIN—GOAL SETTING FOR ANXIETY RESILIENCE

Imagine your life as a road trip. Without a destination, you might end up driving in circles. If you don't have goals, you'll feel like you're moving but not really getting anywhere.

Knowledge is great, but it's what we do with it that really counts. You can read all the self-help books in the world, but if you don't put what you learn into action, you won't see changes.

This is especially crucial in recovery. It's not enough to say, "I want to get better." You need specific, achievable goals, like "I'll attend three support group meetings this week" or "I'll practice my coping skills for 15 minutes each day." Breaking down your big recovery goal into smaller, daily and weekly targets makes the journey less overwhelming.

If you're feeling lost, start setting some goals. Begin small if needed—maybe just make your bed or go for a 10-minute walk. Write your goals down, tell a friend, or stick them on your fridge. Make them real. It's not about being perfect; it's about moving forward. You might stumble sometimes, and that's okay. The key is to keep going, adjusting your goals as needed.

SETTING GOALS FOR DEALING WITH ANXIETY

Setting the right goals is like having a trusty map on a road trip. Here's why it's so important:

DIRECTION AND FOCUS

Imagine you're planning a vacation. If you just say, "I want to go somewhere nice," you might end up anywhere! But if you decide, "I want to visit the Grand Canyon," suddenly you know exactly where you're heading. That's what good goals do for your life. They give you a clear destination, so you're not just wandering around hoping to stumble onto success. When you have a specific target, like "I want to save $2,000 this year," you can make better decisions every day that help you get there.

MOTIVATION AND DRIVE

Let's face it, some days it's hard to get off the couch. But when you have an exciting goal, it's like having your own personal cheerleader. Say you want to run a 5K race. Every time you lace up your shoes to train, you're not just exercising; you're getting closer to crossing that finish line. Good goals turn boring tasks into steps toward something awesome. They encourage you to keep going even during tough times.

ACCOUNTABILITY AND MEASUREMENT

Goals are like a scoreboard for your life. If your goal is to read 12 books this year, you can easily check if you're on track (one book a month) or if you need to step it up. It's satisfying to see your progress, like watching your savings account grow or seeing your running times improve. Plus, when you tell friends or family about your goals, they can cheer you on and maybe give you a nudge if you're slacking off. It's harder to give up when other people know what you're aiming for!

The key is to set goals that are clear, challenging but achievable, and meaningful to you personally. Don't just pick goals because you think you "should"—choose ones that actually excite you. Then break them down into smaller steps, and you've set yourself a road map for success.

WHY DO YOU NEED GOALS IF YOU HAVE ANXIOUS ATTACHMENT?

Setting goals when you have anxious attachment is like giving yourself a safety blanket for your mind.

It helps you feel as if you're more in control. When you have anxious attachment, sometimes it feels like your emotions are on a rollercoaster you can't stop. Having goals is like grabbing the steering wheel of your life. Let's say you decide to learn how to bake the perfect chocolate chip cookie. Suddenly, you have something to focus on that's all about you, not worrying about what others are doing or thinking.

Imagine your partner is out with friends and not texting back right away. Without goals, your mind might start spinning worst-case scenarios. If you're in the middle of a project—like organizing your closet or planning a fun day trip—you've got something positive to keep your thoughts busy. You're less likely to sit and stew in those anxious feelings.

It boosts your self-esteem. Every time you make progress on a goal, it's like giving yourself a high-five. Maybe you're learning to play the guitar. Each new chord you master is proof that you're capable and growing. This helps build confidence from within rather than always seeking approval from others.

It helps you become more independent. Goals help you create your own happiness, separate from your relationships. If you're working toward running your first 5K, you've got something exciting that's just for you. This can make you feel stronger and more self-reliant, even when your partner isn't around.

You'll be able to handle your emotions better. When you're focused on achieving something, it's easier to keep your emotions in check. Let's say you're trying to write a short story. If you get upset about something, you can use your goal as a way to refocus and calm down. "I'll deal with this feeling later; right now, I want to finish this paragraph."

Picture this: It's Saturday night, your partner is at a work event, and they haven't texted in hours. Without goals, you might be glued to your phone, feeling anxious and imagining the worst. But because you set a goal to redecorate your living room, you're busy browsing Pinterest for ideas, measuring your walls for a new painting, and planning a trip to the home décor store. You're so engrossed in your project that when your partner finally calls, you have exciting news to share about your progress.

WHAT ACTIONS DO I TAKE FOR MY DAILY RECOVERY?

Think of recovery like tending a garden. You can't just plant seeds and hope for the best. You need to water, weed, and care for your plants every single day. That's what we're doing with our minds and our attachment style.

So, how do we work on our minds and attachment styles today?

Let's use the SMART technique to make a plan:

- **Specific:** Instead of saying, "I want to feel less anxious," try, "I will practice deep breathing for 5 minutes when I feel anxious about my relationship."

- **Measurable:** Keep a journal where you track how often you use your coping strategies.

- **Attainable:** Start small. Maybe begin with one new habit a week, not ten at once.

- **Relevant:** Choose actions that directly address your anxious attachment. If you struggle with constant texting, your goal might be to wait 30 minutes before responding to nonurgent messages.

- **Time-based:** Set a timeline. "By the end of this month, I will have practiced my new communication skills in at least three conversations with my partner."

Let's picture a day lived intentionally with anxious attachment.

Jean wakes up and reaches for her phone, as usual. Instead of immediately checking if her boyfriend texted, she takes a deep breath and does a quick 5-minute meditation. At work, she feels the urge to text him constantly but remembers her goal. She puts her phone in a drawer and focuses on her tasks, setting a timer to check messages only every two hours.

During lunch, a coworker mentions their upcoming wedding. Usually, this would send Jean into a spiral of "Why isn't my relationship moving faster?" Instead, she congratulates her coworker and then writes in her journal about her feelings, acknowledging them without judgment.

After work, Jean's boyfriend is late for their date. In the past, she might have sent a flurry of worried texts. Today, she uses a grounding technique she learned, focusing on five things she can see, four she can touch, three she can hear, two she can smell, and one she can taste. When he arrives, she calmly expresses her feelings using "I" statements they practiced in couples therapy.

Before bed, Jean reflects on her day, noting in her journal where she used her new skills and where she still struggled. She sets an intention for tomorrow and reminds herself why she's on this journey.

Speaking of which, why are you doing all this?

Remember why you want to recover. Maybe you're tired of the constant anxiety. You want to enjoy your relationships without fear. You dream of feeling secure and confident, whether you're single or partnered.

Recall why you set goals. Goals give you direction. They're like stepping stones across a river, helping you get from where you are to where you want to be. Without them, you might just keep spinning in circles.

Remind yourself why you're working hard every day. Change doesn't happen overnight. It's like building a muscle—you need to exercise it regularly to see results. Each day you practice is a day closer to becoming the secure, confident person you want to be.

On tough days, when you're tempted to fall back into old patterns, ask yourself: "Do I want to feel this way forever, or am I willing to push through discomfort for a better future?" Picture yourself a year from now, more secure and peaceful.

WHAT COULD PREVENT YOU FROM ACHIEVING YOUR GOALS?

Here are some common obstacles that can prevent us from achieving our goals, along with practical ways to overcome them.

LACK OF MOTIVATION

We all have days when we just don't feel like working toward our goals. Maybe you want to get in shape, but going to the gym feels overwhelming.

Instead of an hour-long workout, commit to just 10 minutes of exercise. Getting started is often the hardest part; once you begin, you might want to continue. Also, remind yourself why this goal matters to you. Visualize how good you'll feel after taking action.

FINANCIAL CONSTRAINTS

Let's say you want to start a business but don't have much savings.

Look for low-cost ways to start. Could you begin as a side hustle while keeping your day job? Research small business grants or loans. Consider crowdfunding. Remember, many successful businesses started small and grew over time.

LACK OF TIME

You might want to learn a new skill, like playing guitar, but feel like your schedule is already packed.

Audit your time use. Are you spending hours scrolling social media or watching TV? Replace some of that time with practice. Even 15 minutes a day adds up. Also, try combining activities—could you practice guitar while watching your kid's soccer practice?

SELF-DOUBT

Maybe you want to apply for a promotion at work, but you're not sure you're qualified.

Make a list of your accomplishments and skills. Ask friends or coworkers what they see as your strengths. Remember past challenges you've overcome. If there are skills you're lacking, make a plan to acquire them.

LACK OF FOCUS OR CONCENTRATION

You sit down to work on your goal, like writing a book, but find your mind wandering constantly.

Try the Pomodoro Technique: Work for 25 minutes, then take a 5-minute break. Remove distractions like your phone. Create a dedicated workspace. Use apps that block distracting websites while you work.

FEELING OVERWHELMED

Your goal might seem so big that you don't know where to start. Maybe you want to buy a house, but the process seems daunting.

Break your big goal into smaller, manageable steps. For buying a house, your first step might be to research mortgage options or start saving for a down payment. Celebrate each small win along the way.

LACK OF SUPPORT

You might want to change careers, but your family thinks it's too risky.

Seek out people who support your goals. Join online communities or local groups related to your goal. Consider working with a coach or mentor. Explain your reasoning to skeptical loved ones and ask for their understanding, even if they can't actively support you.

Remember, facing obstacles is a normal part of pursuing any worthwhile goal. The key is to anticipate them, prepare strategies to overcome them, and keep pushing forward even when things get tough. Every step forward, no matter how small, is progress.

FEAR OF FAILURE

Imagine you've always wanted to start a YouTube channel sharing cooking tips, but you're scared no one will watch or you'll embarrass yourself.

Remember that everyone starts somewhere. Your first videos might not be perfect, and that's okay. Look at early videos from successful YouTubers; they often started simple too. Start by sharing videos with just friends and family to build confidence. Remember, failure is often a stepping stone to success—each "failed" video teaches you something.

PROCRASTINATION

You have a goal to declutter your house, but you keep putting it off because it seems like such a big job.

It can be useful to use the "5-minute rule," where you commit to working on something for just five minutes but then often want to continue after you start.

Break the big task into smaller ones—maybe tackle one drawer or shelf at a time. Set a specific time each day for decluttering, like right after dinner. Reward yourself after each session, even if it's just with a favorite snack or TV show.

PERFECTIONISM

Let's say you want to start a blog, but you keep rewriting your first post because it doesn't feel "perfect."

Remind yourself that done is better than perfect. Set a deadline for publishing and stick to it, even if you're not 100% satisfied. Remember that you can always update or improve later. Look at successful blogs and notice that they're not perfect either; they're valuable because they're helpful or interesting, not because they're flawless.

UNEXPECTED SETBACKS

You're training for a marathon, but you twist your ankle and have to take a break from running.

Try to see this as a chance to work on other aspects of your fitness. Maybe you can focus on upper-body strength or flexibility while your ankle heals. Adjust your timeline rather than giving up on your goal entirely. Use the setback as motivation—imagine how satisfying it will be to cross that finish line after overcoming this challenge.

BURNOUT

You're working hard toward a promotion at work, putting in extra hours and taking on additional projects. However, you end up feeling exhausted and losing your passion for the job.

Recognize that self-care is crucial for long-term success. Schedule regular breaks and stick to them. Find ways to make your work more enjoyable—maybe listen to podcasts while doing mundane tasks. Reconnect with why you wanted this promotion in the first place. If possible, delegate some tasks or ask for help. Remember, burning out won't help you reach your goal.

COMPARISON TO OTHERS

You're learning to play guitar, but you feel discouraged because your friend who started at the same time seems to be progressing faster.

Remind yourself that everyone's journey is different. Your friend might have more free time to practice, or maybe they played a similar instrument before. Focus on your own progress—are you better than you were last month? Celebrate your small wins. Use others' success as inspiration rather than discouragement.

LACK OF IMMEDIATE RESULTS

You've started eating healthier and exercising to lose weight, but after two weeks, the scale hasn't budged.

How to overcome it: Remind yourself that significant changes take time. Look for non-scale victories—maybe your energy levels are higher or your clothes fit a bit better. Take progress photos to see small changes the scale might not show. Adjust your expectations to be more realistic; healthy, sustainable weight loss is often slow. Keep a journal to track other benefits you're experiencing, like better sleep or mood improvements.

CHANGING PRIORITIES

You set a goal to learn Spanish, but now you're not sure if it's still relevant to your life.

How to overcome it: It's okay for goals to change. Reflect on why you wanted to learn Spanish initially and whether those reasons are still valid. If not, permit yourself to let this goal go and focus on something more aligned with your current priorities. Or, adjust your goal—maybe instead of fluency, you now aim for basic conversation skills for an upcoming trip.

Remember, the path to achieving our goals is rarely a straight line. It's full of ups and downs, unexpected turns, and sometimes even U-turns. The key is to stay flexible, keep learning from each experience, and never lose sight of why your goal matters to you. Every obstacle you overcome not only brings you closer to your goal but also makes you stronger and more resilient for future challenges.

WHAT TO DO WHEN YOU LACK MOTIVATION

Imagine you've set a goal to exercise three times a week. At first, you're excited and motivated. After a few weeks, you have days where the last thing you want to do is put on your workout clothes.

This is totally normal. Motivation comes and goes like the tide. Some days you'll feel pumped to hit the gym; other days you'd rather stay on the couch. The key is to keep going even when you don't feel like it.

Here's where commitment comes in. It's like a promise you make to yourself. When you commit to something, you decide to do it no matter what, even if you're not in the mood.

Let's say it's a rainy Tuesday evening. You're tired after work, and the thought of going for a run seems awful. This is where you remind yourself: *I committed to running three times this week. It doesn't matter how I feel right now. I'm going to put on my shoes and go.*

The cool thing is, once you start, you often find your mood lifting. Maybe not always, but often enough. You might grumble for the first five minutes of your run, but by the end, you're glad you did it.

This approach works for all kinds of goals:

- Learning a new skill. You committed to practicing guitar for 20 minutes every day. Even if you're not feeling creative, you still pick up the guitar and strum for those 20 minutes.

- You promised yourself to put $50 into savings each payday. Even when you're tempted to spend it on something fun, you stick to your commitment.

- Your goal is to write 500 words a day. Some days the words flow easily; other days it's a struggle. However, you sit down and write anyway, because that's your commitment.

- You decided to cook at home more often to eat healthier. After a long day, takeout seems so tempting. You remember your commitment and whip up a quick, healthy meal instead.

It's okay to not feel motivated all the time. Be kind to yourself on low-energy days. Say something like, "I don't feel like doing this right now, but I'm going to do it anyway because it's important to me."

Over time, this approach builds a powerful habit. You start to rely less on fleeting feelings of motivation and more on your solid commitment. It's like building muscle; the more you practice following through even when you don't feel like it, the easier it becomes.

Action often leads to motivation. By pushing through and doing the thing you committed to, you might just find your motivation sparked again. It's like jump-starting a car— sometimes you need to get moving first before the engine really kicks in.

Next time you're facing a task and your motivation has gone AWOL, remember: It's not about how you feel; it's about what you've committed to do. Take that first small step and let your commitment carry you forward.

KEY TAKEAWAYS

- This chapter introduces the SMART technique (specific, measurable, attainable, relevant, and time-based) for setting effective goals and provides examples of how to apply this technique to manage anxious attachment behaviors.

- Common obstacles to achieving goals include lack of motivation, financial constraints, time limitations, self-doubt, and burnout.

- While motivation is helpful, commitment is more reliable for long-term goal achievement.

- The path to achieving goals is rarely straightforward. It involves setbacks, changing priorities, and the need for flexibility.

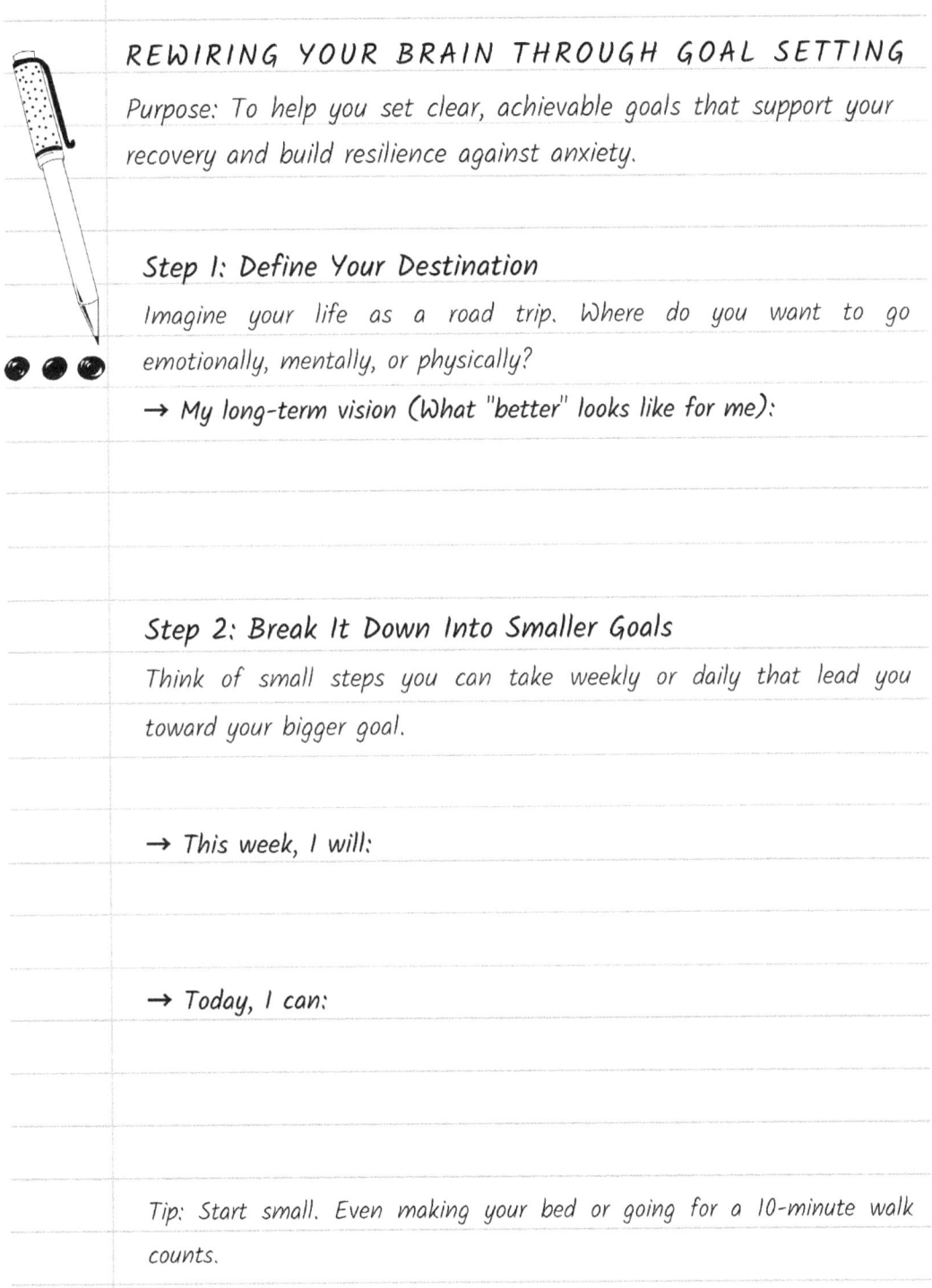

REWIRING YOUR BRAIN THROUGH GOAL SETTING

Purpose: To help you set clear, achievable goals that support your recovery and build resilience against anxiety.

Step 1: Define Your Destination

Imagine your life as a road trip. Where do you want to go emotionally, mentally, or physically?

→ My long-term vision (What "better" looks like for me):

Step 2: Break It Down Into Smaller Goals

Think of small steps you can take weekly or daily that lead you toward your bigger goal.

→ This week, I will:

→ Today, I can:

Tip: Start small. Even making your bed or going for a 10-minute walk counts.

Step 3: Make Your Goals Visible and Accountable

→ Choose one or more of the following:

☐ Write my goals on a sticky note and place it on the fridge/mirror;

☐ Share my goals with a friend, sponsor, or therapist;

☐ Check off completed goals at the end of each day;

☐ Reward myself (small treat or recognition) for following through;

Step 4: Adjust Without Judgment

Stumble? That's okay. Use these questions to recalibrate:

→ What got in the way today?

→ What can I do differently tomorrow?

→ What can I do differently tomorrow?

→ Is my goal still realistic, or do I need to make it smaller or more specific?

Step 5: Weekly Reflection

At the end of the week, reflect:

→ One goal I'm proud to have completed:

→ One thing I want to try again next week:

→ One thing I learned about myself:

Remember:

Progress > Perfection.

You don't need to leap—you just need to keep moving.

STEP 5

YOUR FORTRESS OF CALM—BUILDING BOUNDARIES TO CONQUER ANXIOUS ATTACHMENT

I recently worked with a client named Alex who had a hard time feeling secure in relationships. His story really shows why it's so important to have good boundaries, especially for people with anxious attachment who worry a lot about their relationships.

When Alex first came to see me, he told me about some problems he was having with his girlfriend, Emily. He was always checking his phone for messages from her and would get really worried if she didn't respond quickly. He also kept asking her if everything was okay between them. This kind of behavior usually comes from being afraid of being left or abandoned and needing to feel constantly connected to your partner.

At first, things were good between Alex and Emily. However, as time went on, Alex's need to always be in touch started to become too much for Emily. When she wanted some alone time or to hang out with her friends, Alex would get really upset. He thought it meant she didn't care about him anymore. So he'd send her tons of messages and keep calling her, which only made Emily want to pull away more.

Things came to a head when they had a big argument. Emily told Alex she needed more space. This was a wake-up call for Alex. He realized that the way he was acting might actually ruin their relationship. That's when he decided to get help.

When we started working together, we focused on a few main things:

- We talked about why Alex felt so insecure in relationships. Looking at his past experiences helped him understand his behavior better.

- We worked on ways for Alex to calm himself down when he felt anxious without having to contact Emily. This included things like meditation and changing the way he thought about situations.

- We helped Alex develop his own interests and friendships outside of his relationship. This was hard for him at first, but it helped him feel more independent and confident.

- We practiced how Alex could talk about his feelings in a healthy way while still respecting Emily's needs. We did some role-playing to help with this.

Over time, Alex started to feel much better about himself and his relationship. He learned to give Emily space when she needed it and found that this actually made their time together better. Emily became more affectionate because she didn't feel smothered anymore.

Alex's story shows how important it is to have healthy boundaries in relationships, especially for people who tend to worry a lot about their partners. With some hard work and help, Alex was able to improve his relationship and learn more about himself.

WHAT ARE BOUNDARIES?

Imagine your life is like a house with a garden. Boundaries are like the fences around your garden. They show where your space ends and where others' space begins. Just like a fence protects your garden from stray animals or unwanted visitors, boundaries protect your emotional and physical space from things that might harm you or make you uncomfortable.

Let's say you have a neighbor named Sam. Sam is friendly, but sometimes he comes over unannounced and stays for hours, even when you're busy. Setting a boundary might be telling Sam, "I enjoy your company, but please call before coming over, and you can only visit for an hour on weekdays." This fence helps you manage your time and energy while still being a good neighbor.

There are many types of boundaries we can set in our lives. Time boundaries help us manage our schedules, like saying no to extra work tasks after office hours or not answering work emails on weekends. Physical boundaries protect our personal space, such as asking for distance if someone stands too close or not wanting hugs from people we don't know well. Emotional boundaries help us manage our feelings and energy, like not taking responsibility for others' emotions or letting a friend know when their venting is becoming overwhelming.

We can also set financial boundaries, such as not lending money if it makes us uncomfortable or being clear about what we can afford when planning activities with friends. In the digital world, boundaries might include not sharing your phone password or asking friends not to post pictures of you without permission.

Setting good boundaries is about creating healthier relationships while still connecting with others. It's not about pushing people away. They're saying, "This is what I need to be the best version of myself and the best friend/partner/colleague I can be." It can feel awkward at first, but it gets easier.

WHY YOU NEED TO SET BOUNDARIES WHEN YOU HAVE ANXIOUS ATTACHMENT

If you have anxious attachment, setting boundaries can be really helpful.

When you set boundaries, you're telling yourself, "I know what I need to feel okay." For example, if you know you get worried when your partner goes out with friends, a boundary might be asking them to send you a quick "goodnight" text. This helps you feel secure without asking them to check in all night.

Boundaries also show that you understand what sets off your worries. Maybe you've noticed you feel anxious when plans change suddenly. A boundary could be asking for a bit of advance notice about schedule changes when possible. This isn't about controlling others, but about managing your own feelings better.

When you set boundaries, you're also saying, "This is who I am, and that's okay." Maybe you've always felt like you needed to change yourself to keep others happy. But boundaries let you say, "I need some alone time to recharge" or "I'd like to talk about our relationship once a week." This helps you build your own identity outside of your relationships.

Setting boundaries can feel scary at first, especially if you're worried about pushing people away, but they can actually make relationships stronger. They show that you respect yourself and the other person. It's like saying, "I care about you, and I also care about myself."

Remember, it's okay to start small. Maybe your first boundary is just taking a few deep breaths before responding to a text that makes you anxious. Over time, you'll get more comfortable expressing your needs.

THE TWO GOLDEN QUESTIONS

Knowing your limits in a relationship is like having a personal safety map. It helps you navigate tricky situations and protect your emotional well-being. Two questions can help you draw this map:

WHAT COULD YOUR PARTNER DO TO HURT YOUR ATTACHMENT?

Think about actions or behaviors from your partner that would make you feel insecure, unloved, or disconnected. For example:

- constantly canceling plans at the last minute
- flirting with others in front of you
- belittling your achievements or dreams
- refusing to communicate during conflicts
- keeping secrets or being dishonest

Everyone's list will look different. Maybe you're okay with your partner having close friends of the opposite sex, but constant texting with an ex would cross a line for you. Or perhaps you can handle constructive criticism, but name-calling is an absolute no-go.

Write these down. Be specific. This list is about understanding your own emotional needs and boundaries.

WHAT COULD YOU DO TO HURT YOUR OWN ATTACHMENT?

We often do things that undermine our relationships without realizing it. For example:

- bottling up your feelings instead of communicating

- snooping through your partner's phone because you're insecure

- comparing your relationship to others on social media

- neglecting self-care and becoming overly dependent

- avoiding vulnerability to protect yourself from getting hurt

These behaviors often come from a place of fear or past hurt. Recognizing them is the first step to changing them.

If you understand your personal boundaries and limitations, you can effectively communicate your needs and expectations to your partner.

This awareness also enables you to identify potential warning signs or incompatibilities early in the relationship, and you can deal with potential issues before they become serious.

Healthy relationships have room for both people's needs and boundaries. Your answers to these questions might change over time, and that's okay. The goal is to stay attuned to yourself and your relationship.

SETTING CLEAR BOUNDARIES

Setting clear boundaries in relationships is super important for your well-being and the health of your partnership (Reid, 2024).

BOUNDARIES REGARDING TRIGGERS

These are about recognizing and communicating things that upset you or make you uncomfortable. For example, if you've had bad experiences with alcohol in the past, you might tell your partner, "I don't feel comfortable around heavy drinking. Could we plan more dates that don't involve alcohol?" Or if certain topics are sensitive for you, you could say, "I'd rather not discuss my family situation right now. Can we change the subject?" It's about creating a safe space where you both understand each other's sensitive areas.

BOUNDARIES ON PROXIMITY

This is all about balancing togetherness and independence. Maybe you love your partner but also need your own space. You could say, "I really enjoy our time together, but I also need some alone time to pursue my hobbies and see my friends. How about we each have one night a week for our own activities?" This helps maintain your individual identities within the relationship.

PHYSICAL BOUNDARIES

These boundaries are about your personal space and body. It could be as simple as, "I'm not a big hugger with most people. Is it okay if we stick to handshakes when meeting your friends?" Or in a more intimate context, "I'm ticklish and don't enjoy it. Could we skip the tickling, even in play?" It's about feeling comfortable in your own skin and with physical interactions.

EMOTIONAL BOUNDARIES

This involves protecting your emotional energy and mental health. For instance, if your partner tends to vent a lot about work, you might say, "I want to support you, but hearing about work stress every night is affecting my mood. Could we limit work talk to 15 minutes and then focus on other things?" It's also about not taking responsibility for your partner's emotions. You might need to say, "I care about your happiness, but I can't be solely responsible for it. Have you considered talking to a therapist about these feelings?"

SEXUAL BOUNDARIES

These cover what you're comfortable with in your intimate life, including pace, preferences, and privacy. You might say, "I'm not comfortable sexting. I'd prefer to keep our intimate life to in-person interactions." Or, "I need to build more emotional intimacy before I'm ready for sexual activity. Can we take things slow and check in with each other as we go?" It's also about ongoing consent and communication, like "I appreciate you asking before trying something new in bed. Let's keep checking in with each other like that."

Setting boundaries is an ongoing process. What you're comfortable with might change over time, and that's okay. Keep communicating openly and honestly with your partner.

BOUNDARIES IN A TOXIC RELATIONSHIP

Navigating a relationship with a toxic person, especially for someone with anxious attachment, can be an emotional minefield. Imagine constantly walking on eggshells, never quite sure if your next step will trigger an explosion. This is often the reality for those caught in the grip of a toxic relationship, particularly with someone who exhibits narcissistic traits.

For a person with anxious attachment, this situation can be particularly devastating. Your core fears of abandonment and unworthiness are constantly triggered, keeping you in a state of high alert. The toxic person, whether intentionally or not, plays into these fears. They might shower you with affection one moment, making you feel on top of the world, only to withdraw it without warning the next, leaving you in a tailspin of anxiety and self-doubt. This emotional rollercoaster can be addictive in its intensity, making it hard to break free even when you know the relationship is harmful.

The narcissist's need for admiration and lack of empathy can exacerbate your anxious tendencies. You might find yourself constantly seeking their approval, bending over backward to please them, all while neglecting your own needs and well-being. Your self-esteem, already fragile, takes hit after hit as the toxic person criticizes, belittles, or ignores you. The validation you receive feels as if it's never enough, and it's running out like sand through an hourglass.

In this challenging context, setting boundaries becomes not just important but essential for your mental health and well-being. It's daunting because your anxious attachment style might make you fear that setting boundaries will push the other person away, confirming your worst fears about being unlovable or abandoned. The toxic person may have also conditioned you to put their needs first, making the idea of prioritizing your own needs feel selfish or wrong.

However, you deserve to be treated with dignity. Start small—maybe it's asking for uninterrupted time to speak during conversations or declining plans when you need alone time. Each small boundary you set and maintain is a victory, a step toward reclaiming your power in the relationship.

When communicating your boundaries, be clear and direct, but also prepare for pushback. A toxic person, especially a narcissist, may not readily accept limitations on their behavior. They might try to guilt-trip you, twist your words, or even become angry. This is where having a support system becomes crucial. Reach out to trusted friends, family, or a therapist who can provide encouragement and reality checks when you start to doubt yourself.

Remember, consistency is key. It's not uncommon for someone with anxious attachment to set a boundary and then immediately backtrack out of fear of upsetting the other person. Each time you hold firm, you're not only teaching the other person how to treat you, but you're also proving to yourself that you can tolerate the discomfort of asserting your needs.

As you continue this process, pay close attention to how the toxic person responds to your boundaries over time. Are they making genuine efforts to respect them, or are they constantly pushing against them? Their actions, not their words or promises, will tell you whether this relationship has the potential to become healthier.

Throughout this journey, prioritize self-care and self-compassion. Setting boundaries when you have anxious attachment is hard work. It's okay to struggle, to have setbacks, to feel conflicted. Everything you do to create healthy boundaries is courageous, and you should celebrate even your small victories.

In some cases, you might realize that the toxic person is unwilling or unable to respect your boundaries, no matter how clearly you communicate them. This is when you may need to consider more drastic measures, such as limiting contact or even ending the relationship. While this prospect can be terrifying for someone with anxious attachment, remember that you deserve relationships that nurture and support you, not drain and diminish you.

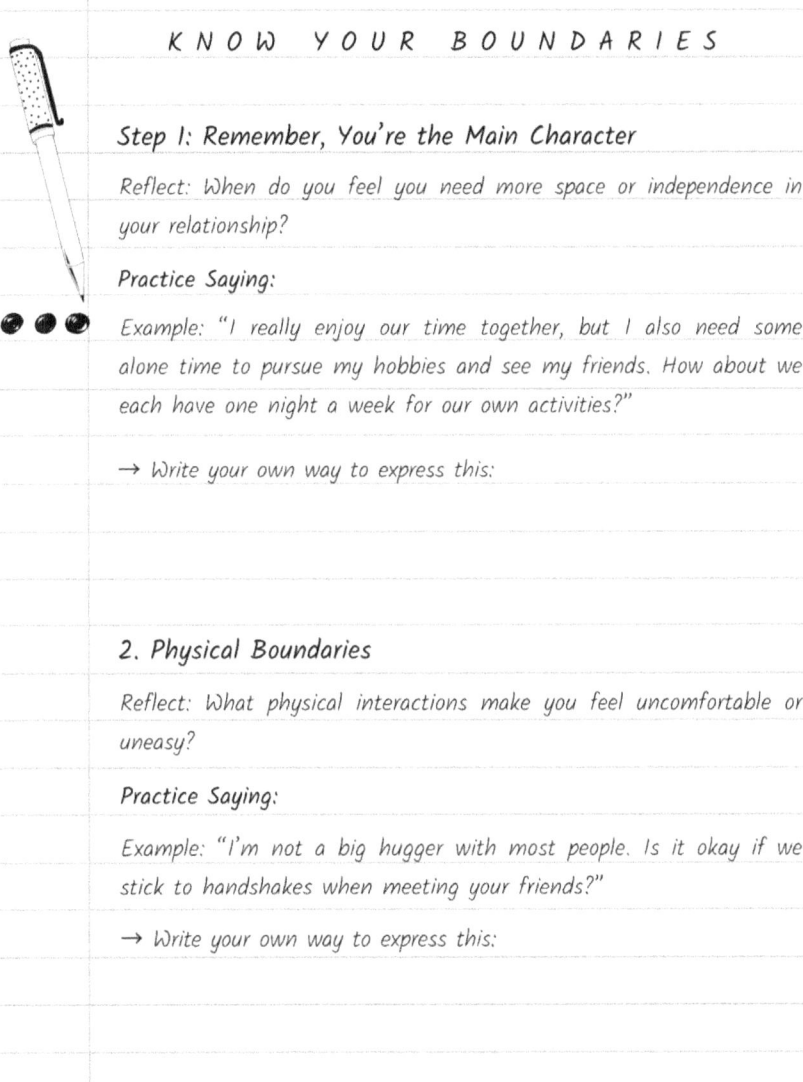

KNOW YOUR BOUNDARIES

Step 1: Remember, You're the Main Character

Reflect: When do you feel you need more space or independence in your relationship?

Practice Saying:

Example: "I really enjoy our time together, but I also need some alone time to pursue my hobbies and see my friends. How about we each have one night a week for our own activities?"

→ Write your own way to express this:

2. Physical Boundaries

Reflect: What physical interactions make you feel uncomfortable or uneasy?

Practice Saying:

Example: "I'm not a big hugger with most people. Is it okay if we stick to handshakes when meeting your friends?"

→ Write your own way to express this:

3. Emotional Boundaries

Reflect: When does your partner's emotional sharing affect your mood or energy negatively?

Practice Saying:

Example: "I want to support you, but hearing about work stress every night is affecting my mood. Could we limit work talk to 15 minutes and then focus on other things?"

→ Write your own way to express this:

4. Sexual Boundaries

Reflect: What makes you feel safe and comfortable in your intimate life? What do you want to avoid?

Practice Saying:

Example: "I'm not comfortable sexting. I'd prefer to keep our intimate life to in-person interactions."

→ Write your own way to express this:

5. Setting Boundaries in Toxic Relationships

Reflect: Have you noticed patterns where your boundaries are pushed or ignored? How does this affect your well-being?

Small Steps:

Write one small boundary you can start with to protect your mental health:

Support System:

Who can you talk to for support when you face pushback or feel unsure?

A CASE STUDY: SARAH AND MIKE'S RELATIONSHIP

Sarah was a 28-year-old graphic designer who had a boyfriend called Mike, a charismatic but toxic partner. Sarah had always struggled with anxious attachment due to childhood trauma and often worried that she wasn't good enough and that people would eventually leave her.

When Sarah first met Mike, she was swept off her feet by his charm and intense attention. He seemed to understand her in a way no one else did, and for a while, Sarah felt like she'd found her perfect match. However, as months passed, Sarah noticed a troubling pattern emerging.

Mike's behavior became unpredictable. Some days, he'd shower her with affection, making grand gestures that left her feeling on top of the world. On other days, he'd become cold and distant, ignoring her calls and messages. When Sarah expressed her concerns, Mike would dismiss them, saying she was being "too sensitive" or "clingy."

This emotional rollercoaster took a toll on Sarah. She found herself constantly anxious, always trying to gauge Mike's mood and adjust her behavior accordingly. She'd cancel plans with friends to be available for Mike, work late to afford the expensive gifts he hinted at wanting, and even change her appearance based on off-hand comments he'd make.

One day, after a particularly hurtful argument where Mike had belittled Sarah's career choices, she reached out to her old friend, Emma. Over coffee, Sarah poured out her heart, describing the relationship's ups and downs. Emma listened patiently, then gently suggested that Mike's behavior seemed toxic and that Sarah might benefit from setting some boundaries.

At first, the idea terrified Sarah. She worried that setting boundaries would push Mike away, confirming her deepest fears of abandonment. However, with her friend's encouragement and the support of a therapist she started seeing, Sarah decided to take small steps toward establishing healthier patterns in her relationship.

She started with something small but meaningful. Mike had a habit of calling her late at night, expecting her to drop everything and listen to him vent about his day. While Sarah wanted to be supportive, these calls often left her exhausted at work the next day. So she decided to set a boundary.

The next time Mike called late, Sarah took a deep breath and said, "Mike, I care about you and want to support you, but I need my sleep to function well at work. Can we agree not to call each other after 10 pm unless it's an emergency? I'd be happy to talk earlier in the evening or schedule a time to catch up tomorrow."

Mike's initial reaction was negative. He accused Sarah of not caring about him and threatened to find someone else who would be there for him. In the past, this would have sent Sarah into a panic, frantically apologizing and giving in. This time, with her support system in place, she stood firm.

"I understand you're upset," she said calmly, "but this boundary is important for my well-being. I hope you can respect that."

To Sarah's surprise, after some initial pushback, Mike grudgingly agreed. This small victory gave Sarah the confidence to set more boundaries. She started saying no to plans she didn't want to participate in, expressed her feelings when Mike made hurtful comments, and carved out time for her hobbies and friendships.

It wasn't easy. There were times when Sarah's anxiety spiked, and she worried she was ruining the relationship. Mike's reactions varied—sometimes he'd respect her boundaries, other times he'd push against them hard. Sarah leaned on her friends, her therapist, and her growing sense of self-worth to stay committed to her boundaries.

Over time, Sarah noticed changes in herself. She felt more confident, less anxious, and more in control of her life. She also noticed changes in her relationship with Mike. As she consistently enforced her boundaries, his behavior began to shift. The emotional highs and lows became less extreme, and he started showing more respect for her needs and feelings.

However, Sarah also realized that some of Mike's toxic behaviors were deeply ingrained. While he made efforts to change, he still struggled with empathy and often prioritized his needs over hers. This realization was painful but also liberating. Sarah understood that she couldn't change Mike—she could only set boundaries and decide what she was willing to accept.

In the end, Sarah made the difficult decision to end the relationship. It was heart-wrenching, and her anxious attachment tendencies made her second-guess herself many times. However, the strength she had gained through setting and maintaining boundaries helped her through the breakup and the healing process that followed.

SELF-REFLECTION EXERCISE

This self-reflection exercise will help you figure out where you might need to set better boundaries. You're encouraged to think about different areas of your life and identify where you feel most stretched or uncomfortable.

WHERE DO I NEED BOUNDARIES?

Grab a notebook or open a notes app on your phone. We're going to make a quick list.

Think about these different areas of your life:

- work or school
- family
- friendships
- romantic relationships
- social media and online life
- personal time and self-care

For each area, ask yourself these questions:

- Do I often feel overwhelmed or stressed in this area?
- Am I doing things I don't really want to do?
- Do I often feel resentful or taken advantage of?
- Do I have trouble saying "no" here?
- Am I ignoring my own needs or feelings to please others?

If you answer "yes" to any of these for an area, write it down. These are potential spots where you might need better boundaries.

Now, for each area you wrote down, think of a specific situation where you felt uncomfortable or stressed. Write a quick note about it.

For example:

Work: Agreed to take on extra projects even though I'm already swamped.

Family: Let mom criticize my career choices without speaking up.

Friends: Always the one planning and organizing hangouts, feeling unappreciated.

Look at your list. Which area stands out the most? Where do you see a pattern of saying "yes" when you want to say "no"?

Pick the area that seems most important or urgent to you right now. This is where you might want to start working on setting better boundaries.

Write down one small step you could take to set a boundary in this area. Keep it simple and doable.

For example:

Work: Next time my boss asks me to take on extra work, I'll say, "I'd love to help, but my plate is full right now. Can we look at my current tasks and prioritize?"

Family: Next time mom brings up my career, I'll say, "I appreciate your concern, but I'm happy with my choices and would rather not discuss this."

Friends: I'll talk to my friends about taking turns planning our get-togethers.

Setting boundaries is a skill that takes practice. Be proud of yourself for any steps you take. It's okay if it feels a bit uncomfortable at first—that's normal when we're making changes.

This exercise is just a starting point. You can come back to it anytime you feel like you need to check in with yourself about your boundaries. The more you practice self-reflection like this, the easier it'll be to spot where you need to set limits and take care of yourself.

THREE WAYS TO SET CLEAR BOUNDARIES

Let's explore three ways to set clear boundaries and see how they play out in a typical day for Jason.

Three ways to set clear boundaries:

1. Be direct and clear in your communication.

2. Follow through with actions that support your words.

3. Respect your own limits and don't feel guilty about them.

Now, let's see how Jason uses these methods in his daily life:

JASON'S BOUNDARY-RESPECTING DAY

Jason wakes up at 7 a.m., feeling refreshed. He's been working on setting and maintaining healthy boundaries, and it's starting to pay off.

At work: Jason's boss approaches him with a last-minute project. Instead of automatically saying yes like he used to, Jason takes a deep breath and says, "I appreciate you thinking of me for this project. However, my schedule is full with the tasks we agreed on yesterday. Which of my current projects would you like me to deprioritize to take this on?" (Method 1: Direct communication)

His boss realizes Jason's plate is indeed full and decides to assign the new project to another team member. Jason feels relieved and proud that he stood up for himself without being rude.

During lunch: Jason's coworker asks if he wants to grab lunch, but Jason had planned to use his break to go for a walk and decompress. He smiles and says, "Thanks for the invite, but I've scheduled some me-time for my lunch break today. Maybe we can plan for lunch together later this week?" (Method 2: Following through with actions)

After work: Jason's phone buzzes with messages from his friends planning a night out. While he enjoys their company, he knows he needs some downtime to recharge. He messages back, "Hey guys, I'm taking tonight for some self-care. Have a great time, and I'll catch up with you this weekend!" (Method 3: Respecting his own limits)

Instead of feeling guilty about not going out, Jason enjoys a quiet evening at home, reading and relaxing.

Before bed: Jason's partner wants to discuss some relationship issues. While Jason cares deeply, he knows he's too tired for a productive conversation. He says, "I want to give this conversation the attention it deserves. Can we set aside time to talk about this tomorrow evening when we're both fresh?" His partner agrees, appreciating Jason's honesty.

As Jason gets ready for bed, he reflects on his day. He realizes that by setting clear boundaries, he's not only taking better care of himself but also improving his relationships. People around him are learning to respect his limits, and he's feeling more balanced and less stressed.

KEY TAKEAWAYS

- This chapter provides a comprehensive explanation of what boundaries are, using metaphors like a house and garden to make the concept more relatable.

- We look at three methods for setting clear boundaries: direct communication, following through with actions, and respecting one's own limits.

PART 4

CONQUERING INSECURITY AND EMBRACING CONFIDENCE

STEP 6

UNLOCKING YOUR VOICE—THE POWER OF EFFECTIVE COMMUNICATION

Zara always worried about her relationship with her boyfriend, Liam. She'd check her phone constantly, wondering why he hadn't texted back yet. Was he upset with her? Had she done something wrong? One day, after hours of imagining worst-case scenarios, Zara decided to do something different. Instead of letting her anxiety spiral, she took a deep breath and called Liam.

"Hey, can we talk?" she asked nervously. "I've been feeling really anxious lately about our relationship, and I think I need to explain what's going on in my head."

To Zara's surprise, Liam listened patiently as she poured out her fears and insecurities. He hadn't realized how much she was struggling and was grateful she opened up to him. Together, they talked about ways to make Zara feel more secure, like setting up regular check-ins and being clearer about their plans.

This conversation was a turning point for Zara. She realized that by communicating her needs clearly, she could actually address her anxieties instead of letting them fester. It wasn't always easy, but each time she chose to talk things out instead of worrying in silence, she felt a little bit stronger.

Zara's story shows us how powerful good communication can be. By speaking up, she gave Liam a chance to understand and respond to her needs. It didn't magically fix everything, but it was the first step toward a healthier, more secure relationship—for both of them.

COMMUNICATING EFFECTIVELY

Think about the last time you felt frustrated with someone close to you. Maybe your partner forgot an important date, or your friend kept interrupting you during a conversation. How did you handle it? Did you stay quiet and hope they'd figure it out on their own? Or did you speak up?

These situations are common in our daily lives, and how we respond to them can significantly impact our relationships. Many of us tend to bottle up our feelings, expecting others to somehow intuitively understand what's bothering us. The truth is people can't read our minds. No matter how well someone knows us, they can't always guess what we're thinking or feeling. That's where communication comes in. It's like building a bridge between your world and theirs.

When we talk about our needs, thoughts, emotions, or boundaries, we're giving others a chance to understand us better. It's like handing them a map to navigate our inner world. Without this map, they might accidentally step on our toes or miss important landmarks. For example, if your partner forgets your anniversary, they might not realize how much it hurts you unless you express it. Your friend who keeps interrupting might not be aware of how it makes you feel unheard and undervalued.

Effective communication doesn't mean you have to give long speeches or use fancy words. Sometimes it's as simple as saying, "I feel hurt when you do that" or "I'd really appreciate it if you could help me with this task." These straightforward statements can be powerful tools for improving understanding and strengthening relationships.

For example, if you're feeling overwhelmed at work, telling your partner, "I need some quiet time when I get home," gives them a clear way to support you. They can't offer this help if they don't know you need it. Similarly, telling your friend, "I feel frustrated when I'm interrupted. Could we try taking turns to speak?" provides them with specific feedback and a solution to improve your conversations.

It might feel scary at first, especially if you're not used to speaking up. You might worry about hurting someone's feelings or causing conflict. However, the more you practice, the easier it gets. Start with small, low-stakes situations. Express appreciation for something someone did, or politely ask for a small favor. As you become more comfortable, you can tackle more challenging conversations.

The results of improved communication can be amazing. Relationships often improve as misunderstandings decrease. You might find yourself feeling more confident and understood. Your loved ones may appreciate knowing how to support you better. It's like turning on a light in a dark room—suddenly, everything becomes clearer and easier to navigate.

Remember, communication is a two-way street. It's not just about talking; it's also about listening (Robinson et al., 2024). When others share their thoughts and feelings with you, pay attention. Ask questions if you're not sure about something. This back-and-forth creates stronger connections and helps everyone feel heard and valued.

Active listening is a crucial part of effective communication. It's about really concentrating on what is being said and showing the speaker that their thoughts and feelings matter to you. This will help you have more meaningful conversations.

Here are some tips for active listening:

- Put away distractions and give the speaker your full attention.

- Use cues like nodding or maintaining eye contact to show that you're listening to the speaker.

- Provide feedback: Summarize what you've heard to ensure you've understood correctly.

- Don't interrupt: Let the other person finish their thoughts before responding.

- Respond appropriately: Be honest and respectful in your response.

By combining clear expression of your own thoughts and feelings with active listening, you create a communication cycle that strengthens your relationships. It's like a dance where both partners need to be in sync for it to work smoothly.

Of course, effective communication doesn't mean always agreeing with each other. Disagreements are a normal part of any relationship. The key is how you handle these disagreements. When you communicate openly and respectfully, even conflicts can become opportunities for growth and deeper understanding.

For instance, if you and your partner disagree about how to spend your weekend, instead of arguing or giving in resentfully, you could say something like, "I understand you want to relax at home, and I want to go out. How about we compromise? We could stay in on Saturday and go out on Sunday." This approach acknowledges both perspectives and seeks a solution that works for everyone.

Remember, good communication is a skill, and like any skill, it improves with practice. There will be times when you stumble or say the wrong thing, and that's okay. What's important is that you keep trying. Each conversation is an opportunity to learn and improve.

To communicate effectively, you also need to understand the emotions and intentions behind the information. By learning to communicate clearly about your own needs and feelings and listening actively to others, you can improve your relationships, reduce conflicts, and create a more harmonious environment in all areas of your life.

WHAT HAPPENS IF I DON'T COMMUNICATE?

So, what happens when we don't speak up about our feelings or needs? It's like trying to hold a beach ball underwater; eventually, it's going to pop up, and probably not when you want it to. This analogy captures the unpredictable and often explosive nature of suppressed emotions and unmet needs.

Imagine this: Your roommate Tom keeps leaving dirty dishes in the sink. At first, you think, *It's not a big deal. I don't want to make a fuss.* As days go by, the dishes pile up, and your frustration grows. You find yourself getting annoyed at little things Tom does, even if they're unrelated to the dishes. One day, he asks to borrow your charger, and suddenly you snap, yelling about how inconsiderate he is. Tom is shocked, and you feel guilty for overreacting. This is what can happen when we don't communicate—we lose control and react badly when we least expect it.

This scenario is all too familiar for many of us. We've all been in situations where we've bitten our tongues to keep the peace, only to find ourselves exploding over something seemingly minor later on. It's like a pressure cooker—the steam builds up over time and, eventually, it has to release.

When we keep our feelings bottled up, it can also make us feel anxious and insecure. You might start wondering, *Am I being unreasonable? Should I just deal with it?* This inner conflict can leave you feeling lonely, even when you're surrounded by people. You might start to withdraw, thinking no one understands you.

Let's expand on this a bit. Imagine you're at work, and your colleague keeps taking credit for your ideas in meetings. At first, you brush it off, thinking it's not worth making a fuss about. But as it continues, you start to doubt yourself. *Maybe my ideas aren't as good as I thought*, you might think. Or *Am I just being too sensitive?* This self-doubt can start to seep into other areas of your life. You might become hesitant to speak up in meetings, or you might start second-guessing your decisions in other areas.

Not communicating can lead to a lot of misunderstandings too. In our example with Tom, he might think you're angry about the charger when really it's about the dishes. He can't fix a problem he doesn't know exists. This can create a cycle of confusion and hurt feelings on both sides.

Think about a time when a friend seemed upset with you, but you had no idea why. Maybe they were giving you the cold shoulder or making passive-aggressive comments. You rack your brain trying to figure out what you did wrong, but come up empty. This situation is frustrating for both parties—your friend is upset about something you did, but because they haven't communicated it, you're left in the dark and unable to address the issue.

So, what could you do instead? In the case with Tom, you could say something like, "Hey Tom, I've noticed the dishes are piling up. Could we come up with a system to keep the kitchen cleaner?" This opens up a conversation where both of you can express your needs and find a solution together.

Speaking up doesn't mean being confrontational. It's about being clear and honest in a respectful way. It might feel uncomfortable at first, but it's much better than letting things build up until they explode. By communicating, you're giving yourself and others the chance to understand and make things better.

Let's look at another example. Say you're in a romantic relationship, and your partner has a habit of making plans without consulting you first. You've always gone along with it to avoid conflict, but it's starting to make you feel like your time and opinions don't matter. Instead of letting this resentment build, you could say something like, "I appreciate that you're making plans for us, but I'd really like to be involved in the decision-making process. Could we discuss our plans together before committing to them?"

This approach does several things:

- It acknowledges your partner's positive intention (making plans for you both).

- It clearly expresses your feelings and needs.

- It suggests a solution that could work for both of you.

By communicating this way, you're not attacking your partner or making them defensive. Instead, you're inviting them to work with you on improving your relationship.

Of course, speaking up isn't always easy. Many of us have been conditioned to avoid conflict or to prioritize others' feelings over our own. We might worry about coming across as selfish or causing problems. By not communicating, aren't we actually causing more problems in the long run?

Think about it this way: If you had a pebble in your shoe, would you keep walking on it, getting more and more uncomfortable, or would you stop and remove it? Not speaking up about our needs or feelings is like choosing to walk on that pebble. Sure, you might avoid the momentary discomfort of stopping and taking off your shoe, but you're setting yourself up for a much more painful journey.

Learning to communicate effectively is a skill, and like any skill, it takes practice. Start small. Maybe you begin by expressing appreciation more often: "I really liked how you handled that situation" or "Thanks for doing the grocery shopping; it helped me out." These positive communications can make it easier to bring up more difficult topics later.

When you do need to address a problem, try using "I" statements. Instead of "You always leave your stuff everywhere," try "I feel frustrated when the living room is messy. Could we work on keeping it tidy together?" This approach focuses on your feelings and a potential solution, rather than placing blame.

Remember, effective communication isn't just about talking; it's also about listening. When you open up a dialogue, be prepared to hear the other person's perspective too. They might have needs or feelings they haven't expressed either.

In the end, clear and honest communication is about respect—respect for yourself and your own needs and respect for others and their right to understand how their actions affect you. It's about creating an environment where everyone feels heard and valued.

So the next time you find yourself holding that beach ball underwater, take a deep breath and consider letting it rise to the surface gently. You might be surprised at how much lighter you feel and how much stronger your relationships can become when you're all swimming in the same clear waters.

SIX GOLDEN RULES OF EFFECTIVE COMMUNICATION

Good communication can transform your relationships and make life so much smoother. It's not always that easy. We've all had those moments where we're trying to express ourselves and it comes out all wrong, or we bottle things up until we explode. With a little practice, anyone can become a better communicator.

As we said before, speak up about your feelings and needs. We often expect others to just know what we want. Unfortunately, your partner can't magically know you need a hug after a tough day or that you're feeling neglected because they've been working late all week. You've got to put it out there. Try saying something like, "Hey, I've had a rough day and could really use a hug," or "I'm feeling a bit lonely lately. Could we plan a date night this week?" It could feel awkward at first, but it will get easier.

You also have to be able to share your thoughts openly. Our minds are constantly whirring with ideas, worries, and reactions. Letting others in on what's going on up there can help them understand you better. For example, if your friend cancels plans at the last minute, instead of just saying "It's fine" (when it's not), try explaining your thought process: "When you canceled, I started thinking you might not value our friendship as much as I do. I know that's probably not true, but it's where my mind went."

Setting clear boundaries is another crucial part of good communication. Think of it as drawing a line in the sand—not to keep people out, but to show them where they can safely step. For example, if you're not a fan of surprise visits, you could say, "I really enjoy spending time with you, but unexpected visits stress me out. Could you give me a heads up before coming over?" This way, you're not attacking the other person, just explaining what works for you.

Making your communication personal is like adding your signature to a message. Instead of making general statements or complaints, focus on your own experiences and feelings. Rather than saying, "You're always late," try, "I feel like you don't care about me when you are late. Can you try a little bit harder to be on time?" This approach is less likely to put others on the defensive and more likely to lead to productive conversations.

Being straightforward is all about cutting through the noise and getting to the heart of the matter. No need for complicated word games or subtle hints. If you're upset that your roommate ate your leftovers, don't leave passive-aggressive notes on the fridge. Just say, "Hey, I was looking forward to eating that pasta for lunch. In the future, could you ask before eating my food?" Being direct is not about being mean; it just means making yourself clear to other people.

Finally, remember to keep your communication warm and kind (Burton, 2024). You can be honest about your feelings without being harsh. Instead of snapping, "You never help around here!" try, "I'm feeling a bit overwhelmed with housework lately. I'd really appreciate some help. Could we divide up the chores?" This approach is more likely to lead to a positive outcome and keeps the lines of communication open.

THE SIX GOLDEN RULES OF EFFECTIVE COMMUNICATION

Practice expressing your needs, emotions, and boundaries clearly, authentically, and effectively.

1. Speak Up About Your Feelings and Needs

What are you feeling or needing, but haven't said out loud?

How could you express this need or emotion clearly?

Example: "I had a rough day and could really use a hug."

2. Share What's on Your Mind

What thought has been bothering you that you haven't shared?

How could you express this thought honestly, yet kindly?

Example: "When you canceled our plans, I felt like maybe you don't value our friendship."

3. Set Clear Boundaries

What boundary would you like to set in your relationships?

How could you express this boundary calmly and clearly?

Example: "I love seeing you, but surprise visits stress me out."

4. Make It Personal

Think of a recent situation where you made a general complaint.

Rephrase it using your personal experience.

Example: "I feel unimportant when you're late. Could you try to be on time?"

A CASE FOR DISCUSSION

As I glanced at my schedule for the day, I noticed Stela was due for her session in 15 minutes. She was a bright and hardworking person, but had been struggling with work-life balance, often canceling or arriving late to our sessions. Today, I decided, was the day to address this pattern head-on.

When Stela rushed in, 15 minutes late and already apologizing, I greeted her with a warm smile. "Stela, I'm glad you made it today," I began, keeping my tone welcoming despite the lateness. I knew that what I was about to do might be challenging for both of us, but it was necessary for Stela's progress and our therapeutic relationship.

"Before we start, there's something important I'd like to discuss. Is that okay with you?" I asked, making sure to get her consent before proceeding. When she nodded, looking a bit apprehensive, I took a deep breath and focused on expressing my thoughts and feelings clearly.

"I've noticed a pattern of last-minute cancellations and late arrivals to our sessions," I said, careful to keep my tone free of judgment. "When this happens, I feel concerned about the consistency of our work together and worried that you might not be getting the full benefit of therapy."

I paused, allowing Stela to take in what I'd said. I could see a flicker of guilt cross her face, but I continued, knowing it was important to fully express my thoughts.

"I understand that work is demanding," I acknowledged, showing empathy for her situation. "But I'm wondering if these frequent disruptions might be related to the issues we've been discussing about setting boundaries and prioritizing self-care."

Now came the part where I needed to set a clear boundary. I reminded myself that this was not just for my benefit but for Stela's as well. "Moving forward, I'd like us to commit to our scheduled session times," I said firmly but kindly. "If you absolutely must cancel, I need at least 24 hours' notice. This helps me manage my schedule and ensures that our time together is protected. How does that sound to you?"

I watched Stela carefully as I said this, noting her body language and facial expressions. She seemed to be listening intently, which encouraged me to continue.

Adding a personal touch, I said, "As your therapist, I'm invested in your progress and well-being. When our sessions are irregular, it's harder for us to maintain the continuity that's so important for effective therapy."

I wanted to be direct about finding a solution, so I asked, "Can we work together to find a way to prioritize these sessions, even when work gets hectic? Perhaps we could explore strategies to help you communicate your needs to your employer or find ways to manage your time more effectively?"

Throughout this conversation, I made a conscious effort to keep my tone warm and supportive. I wanted to demonstrate that setting boundaries and expressing needs can be done with kindness.

When Stela responded, admitting her struggle to say no at work, I felt a sense of breakthrough. "Thank you for sharing that, Stela," I said, my voice filled with encouragement. "It takes courage to acknowledge these challenges. In our future sessions, let's focus on developing those communication and boundary-setting skills at work. This could help not only with maintaining our therapy schedule but also with the work-life balance issues you've been facing."

As our session ended, I felt satisfied with how the conversation had gone. We had a plan moving forward, and more importantly, I had modeled effective communication for Stela. I hoped that this experience would not only improve our therapeutic relationship but also provide Stela with valuable skills she could apply in her daily life.

After Stela left, I took a moment to reflect. These conversations are never easy, but they're essential for meaningful progress in therapy. By expressing my needs clearly, setting boundaries, and maintaining a supportive atmosphere, I turned a potential conflict into an opportunity for growth.

KEY TAKEAWAYS

- This chapter outlines six "golden rules" of effective communication: expressing emotional needs, sharing thoughts openly, setting clear boundaries, making communication personal, being direct, and maintaining warmth and kindness in interactions.

- The consequences of poor communication include misunderstandings, emotional outbursts, and increased anxiety. It stresses that not communicating can lead to bottled-up feelings and unresolved issues in relationships.

STEP 7

A NEW BEGINNING—TIPS FOR DATING AFTER HEALING

Elsa stood in front of her mirror, adjusting her blue scarf with a sense of calm excitement. She was about to head out for a first date, and as she looked at her reflection, she couldn't help but marvel at how far she'd come. Just two years ago, Elsa had been nursing the wounds of a painful breakup that had left her feeling lost and insecure. Her relationship with Eric had been a rollercoaster of highs and lows, filled with arguments and misunderstandings. When it ended, Elsa felt like she'd lost a part of herself.

Today was different. Elsa felt a quiet confidence that came from within, a result of the hard work she'd put into healing and understanding herself. Through therapy, journaling, and self-reflection, Elsa had gained valuable self-awareness. She now understood that she had an anxious attachment style, which had made her prone to worrying about abandonment. In her relationship with Eric, this manifested as clinginess and a constant need for reassurance.

One of Elsa's biggest breakthroughs was understanding her role in her past relationship's problems. She realized she had often expected Eric to read her mind instead of communicating her needs clearly. This realization had led her to work hard on expressing herself more clearly and listening actively. She felt prepared to have open, honest conversations about expectations and feelings in her future relationships.

Learning to set and maintain healthy boundaries was another important part of Elsa's journey. In the past, she had often sacrificed her own needs to please others. *I remember canceling plans with friends just because Eric asked me to hang out last minute*, Elsa thought. *Now I know it's okay to say no and to have my own life alongside a relationship.*

As part of her healing process, Elsa developed a solid self-care routine that helped her maintain emotional balance. She had a regular jogging routine, enjoyed painting, and had cultivated a close circle of friends she could rely on. These activities and relationships formed the foundation of a life she truly loved. *My happiness doesn't depend on being in a relationship anymore*, Elsa realized. *I've built a life I love, and a partner would be an addition to that, not the center of it.*

Through her healing journey, Elsa also became clear about her values and what she wanted in a partner. She knew she valued honesty, emotional openness, and shared interests in art and nature. This clarity gave her a sense of purpose in her dating life. *I'm not just looking for anyone to fill a void*, Elsa thought. *I know what's important to me in a relationship, and I'm willing to wait for the right match.*

As Elsa grabbed her keys and headed out the door, she felt a mix of excitement and calm. She knew that regardless of how this date went, she was in a good place. She had done the work to understand herself, heal from past hurts, and build a fulfilling life.

Elsa wasn't just starting a date; she was stepping into a new chapter of her life, one where she was fully prepared to give and receive love in a healthy, fulfilling way.

HOW DO YOU KNOW YOU'RE READY FOR AUTHENTIC LOVE?

Have you ever wondered if you're truly ready to dive back into the dating pool? Not just for any relationship, but for one that's genuine, healthy, and authentic? Here are some signs that you might be ready to love authentically.

YOU'RE AWARE OF YOUR ATTACHMENT STYLE

Remember how you used to cling to your partner, always fearing they'd leave? Or maybe you were the one who'd push people away when they got too close? That's your attachment style at work.

Being ready for authentic love means you've done some soul-searching. You understand whether you're anxious, avoidant, or securely attached. More importantly, you know how this affects your relationships.

For example, if you realize you have an anxious attachment style, you might catch yourself wanting to text your date constantly. However, now, instead of giving in to that urge, you can take a deep breath and remind yourself that it's okay to give them space.

YOU TRUST YOUR RECOVERY PROCESS

When you're ready for authentic love, you trust the work you've done on yourself.

Maybe you've been to therapy, read self-help books, or spent time journaling. Whatever your path, you feel confident in the progress you've made. You're not perfect, but you're not the same person you were before.

You might think, *I know I've grown because I can now talk about my ex without feeling angry or sad. I've learned from that relationship and I'm ready to apply those lessons*.

YOU FEEL SAFE ALONE AND WITH OTHERS

Remember when being alone felt like punishment? Or when someone showing interest in you sent you into a panic? Those days are behind you now.

Being ready for authentic love means you're comfortable in your own company. You enjoy your hobbies, your friends, and your work. You don't need a relationship to feel complete.

At the same time, you're not scared when someone shows interest in you. You can think, *Oh, that person seems nice*, without immediately worrying about all the ways it could go wrong.

YOUR EMOTIONAL REACTIONS HAVE CHANGED

Think back to how you used to react in relationships. Maybe you'd burst into tears if your partner was 10 minutes late, assuming they'd been in a terrible accident (or worse, cheating!). Or perhaps you'd shut down completely if there was any hint of conflict.

Now, things are different. You still have emotions (you're human, after all), but they do not control you.

For instance, if your date cancels plans, you might feel disappointed. Instead of spiraling into self-doubt or anger, you can think, *That's a shame. I was looking forward to seeing them. I'll check if we can reschedule, and if not, I'll enjoy a night to myself.*

AM I READY FOR AUTHENTIC LOVE?

Not just any relationship — but one that's real, reciprocal, and emotionally safe.

1. You Know Your Attachment Style

Have you identified how you tend to connect (or disconnect) in relationships?

☐ I recognize when my anxiety or avoidance is showing up;

☐ I can pause before reacting impulsively;

☐ I've learned healthier ways to self-soothe;

Reflection Prompt:

- What does your attachment style sound like in your head?

Write a sentence your inner voice says in moments of relational stress.

Example: "If they don't reply quickly, maybe I did something wrong."

2. You Trust Your Healing Work

You've done inner work. You've reflected. You've grown.

☐ I've taken responsibility for my past patterns;

☐ I can talk about previous relationships without feeling stuck in pain;

☐ I believe I'm capable of choosing differently now;

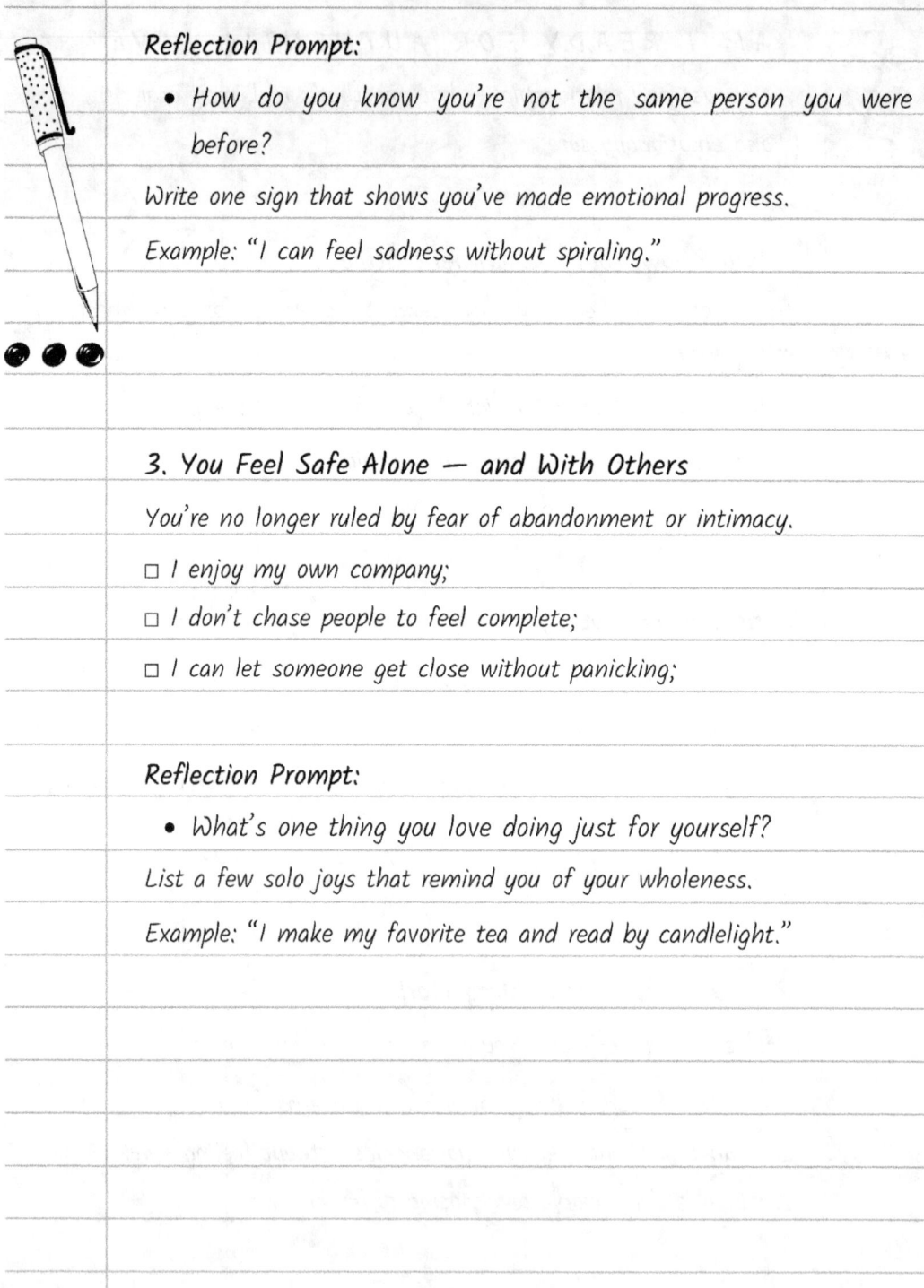

Reflection Prompt:

- *How do you know you're not the same person you were before?*

Write one sign that shows you've made emotional progress.

Example: "I can feel sadness without spiraling."

3. You Feel Safe Alone — and With Others

You're no longer ruled by fear of abandonment or intimacy.

☐ *I enjoy my own company;*

☐ *I don't chase people to feel complete;*

☐ *I can let someone get close without panicking;*

Reflection Prompt:

- *What's one thing you love doing just for yourself?*

List a few solo joys that remind you of your wholeness.

Example: "I make my favorite tea and read by candlelight."

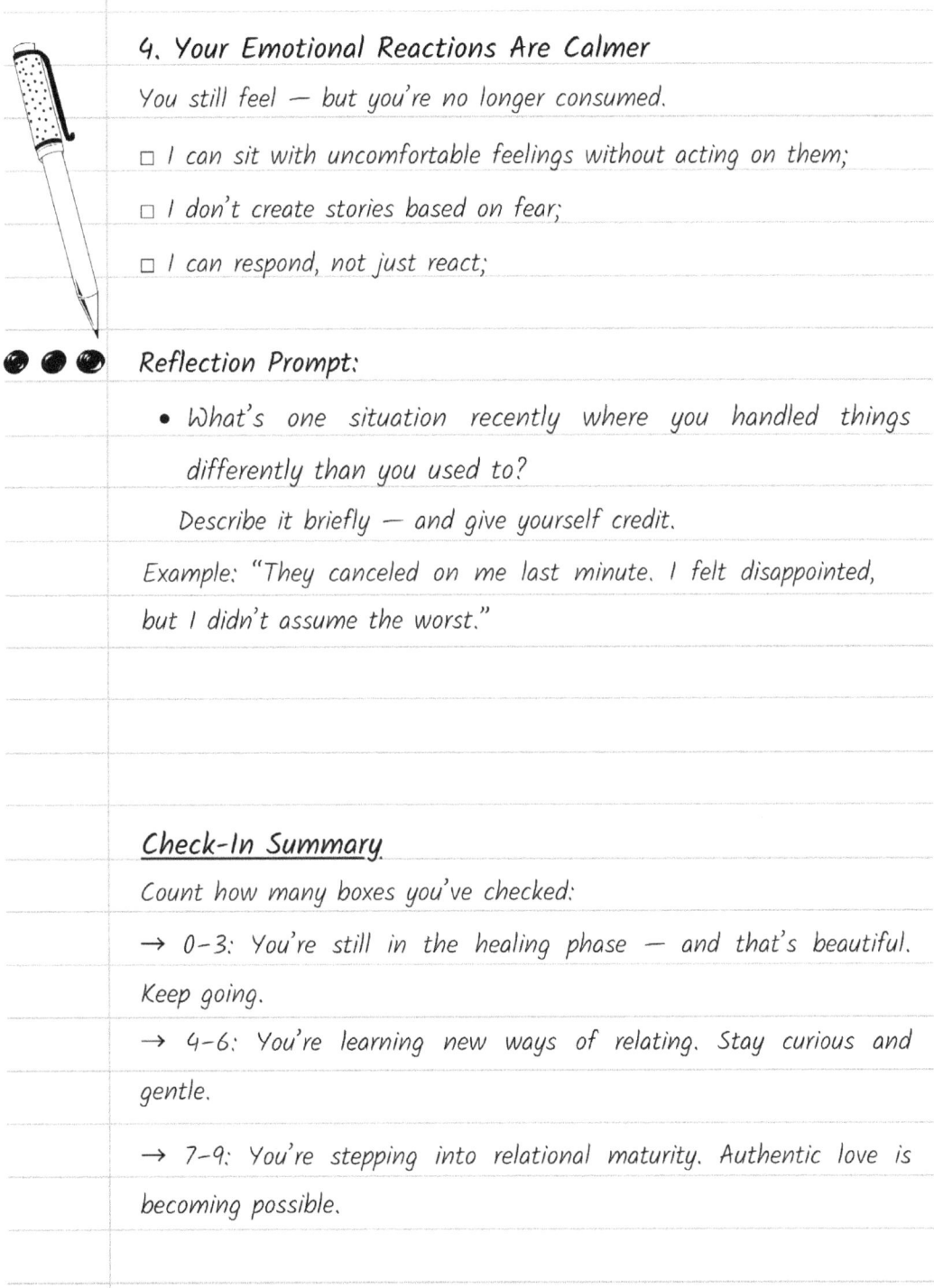

4. Your Emotional Reactions Are Calmer

You still feel — but you're no longer consumed.

☐ I can sit with uncomfortable feelings without acting on them;

☐ I don't create stories based on fear;

☐ I can respond, not just react;

Reflection Prompt:

- What's one situation recently where you handled things differently than you used to?

  Describe it briefly — and give yourself credit.

Example: "They canceled on me last minute. I felt disappointed, but I didn't assume the worst."

Check-In Summary

Count how many boxes you've checked:

→ 0-3: You're still in the healing phase — and that's beautiful. Keep going.

→ 4-6: You're learning new ways of relating. Stay curious and gentle.

→ 7-9: You're stepping into relational maturity. Authentic love is becoming possible.

Final Prompt

What does "authentic love" mean to you?

Write your own definition — not what you were told to believe,

but what feels true now.

PUTTING IT ALL TOGETHER

Being ready for authentic love doesn't mean you're perfect or you'll never face challenges in relationships. What it does mean is that you're equipped to handle those challenges in a healthier way.

You understand yourself better. You trust your ability to cope with difficulties. You're comfortable being single and open to being with someone. You can manage your emotions without letting them manage you.

If you recognize these signs in yourself, you're ready to open yourself up to authentic love. Remember, the goal isn't to find someone to complete you, but to share your already complete self with someone else.

It's also fine if you're not quite there yet. Keep working on yourself, growing, and trusting that you're on the right path. Authentic love is worth the wait and the work.

A FRESH START: CHOOSING A PARTNER AFTER PERSONAL GROWTH

You've done the hard work. You've looked inside yourself, faced your fears, and grown in ways you never thought possible. Now, as you stand at the threshold of a new chapter in your life, you might be wondering: *How do I choose a partner who will complement the new, improved me?*

Let's start by taking a trip down memory lane, but not for nostalgia's sake. Grab a pen and paper or open a note on your phone, and make a list of the mistakes you made in past relationships. Maybe you always went for the emotionally unavailable type, or perhaps you ignored red flags because you were afraid of being alone. Maybe you tried to change your partners instead of accepting them, or you didn't communicate your needs clearly. Whatever your patterns were, write them down. This isn't about beating yourself up—it's about learning and growing.

Now, here's where it gets interesting: Your mission, should you choose to accept it, is to do the opposite of what didn't work before. Think of it as a relationship version of opposite day. If you always went for the "bad boy" or "party girl" type, try giving that quiet, reliable person a chance. If you used to ignore your own needs to please your partner, make a pact with yourself to speak up about what you want. If you used to jump into relationships quickly, try taking things slow and really getting to know someone first. Remember, the goal isn't to completely change who you are or what you're attracted to. It's about making conscious choices rather than falling into old habits.

You've learned a lot through your recovery process, and now it's time to put that knowledge into action. If you've discovered that you need alone time to recharge, look for a partner who respects that and doesn't take it personally. If you've realized that open communication is important to you, pay attention to how potential partners express themselves. If you've found that shared values are crucial for your happiness, don't be afraid to have those important conversations early on.

When it comes to attachment styles, you have two great options. You can look for someone with a secure attachment style; these people tend to be comfortable with intimacy, good at communicating, and able to handle conflict in a healthy way. They're like the golden retrievers of the dating world—friendly, reliable, and drama-free! Alternatively, consider someone who's aware of their attachment issues and is actively working on them. We're all works in progress, right? Someone who's committed to personal growth can be a great partner because they understand the importance of self-improvement and are likely to support your journey too.

So how do you spot these people? Look for signs like openness about feelings and past experiences, consistency in words and actions, respect for boundaries (both yours and their own), willingness to have deep, meaningful conversations, and the ability to take responsibility for their actions without playing the blame game. These are good indicators that you're dealing with someone who's either securely attached or on their way there.

Remember, choosing a partner after recovery is about being intentional and true to yourself. It's not about finding a perfect person (they don't exist!) but about finding someone who's a good fit for the healthier, more self-aware you. Trust your gut feeling, and take your time before committing to anything. Keep working on yourself, because a healthy relationship involves two people who continue to grow, both together and independently. Be honest about your past and your journey; the right person will appreciate your self-awareness and the work you've done.

BE YOUR AUTHENTIC SELF

Many of us with anxious attachment styles have spent years hiding our true selves. We've buried our needs, masked our insecurities, and pretended to be more independent than we really are. But here's the truth: There's incredible power in being honest about who you are and what you need.

When you hide your attachment needs, you're not just deceiving others; you're also denying yourself. You push down your desire for closeness, your fear of abandonment, and your need for reassurance. But those needs don't disappear just because you ignore them. Instead, they often come out in unhealthy ways, leading to clingy behavior, emotional outbursts, or silent resentment.

There's another way. It starts with being honest—with yourself and with others. Acknowledge your needs. Accept your experiences. Embrace your attachment style as a part of who you are.

This honesty isn't always easy. It can feel scary to admit that you need more support or reassurance than others might. You might be worried that you'll push people away if you're open about your anxious attachment issues. You might worry that being open about your anxious attachment will push people away. In reality, the opposite often happens.

When you're honest about who you are:

- You free yourself from the exhausting task of constant pretense.

- You open the door to deeper, more authentic connections.

- You give others the chance to meet your needs—needs they might not have known about before.

- You start to heal the parts of yourself that have been neglected or hidden.

Remember, your needs are valid. Your experiences have shaped you. By acknowledging these truths, you're not being needy or weak—you're being authentic and brave.

This journey toward honesty and self-acceptance isn't always smooth. There might be setbacks. Some people might not understand. With each step toward authenticity, you're moving toward healthier relationships and a more integrated sense of self.

BE YOUR AUTHENTIC SELF

If you've spent years hiding your true needs, you're not alone.

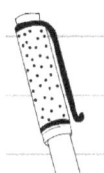

Anxious attachment can make you feel like your needs are "too much." Maybe you've learned to:

- Pretend to be more independent than you are
- Swallow your need for closeness
- Hide your fears of being abandoned

But here's the truth: Hiding doesn't heal. Honesty does. Your needs don't vanish when ignored—they often come out in painful or confusing ways.

Why authenticity matters:

- When you're honest about who you are:
- You stop managing an exhausting emotional performance
- You create room for real connection
- You give others the chance to support you
- You start healing neglected parts of yourself

Reflection: What have you been hiding?

Take a deep breath. Gently answer the prompts below.

1. What parts of yourself do you tend to hide in relationships?

(e.g., my need for reassurance, my fear of being alone)

- _____
- _____

2. What do you wish you could say out loud, but often don't?

(to a partner, friend, or even yourself)

- "I feel scared when I don't hear from you."
- "I need more closeness than I let on."
- _____

3. What might change if you were just 10% more honest?

- _____
- _____

Mini Practice: Speak One Small Truth

This week, pick one small, honest thing you can share with someone safe. Start small. You don't have to overshare. Just one step toward authenticity.

- I will tell _____
- that I feel _____

Example: "Sometimes I act like I'm fine, but I actually need more reassurance than I admit."

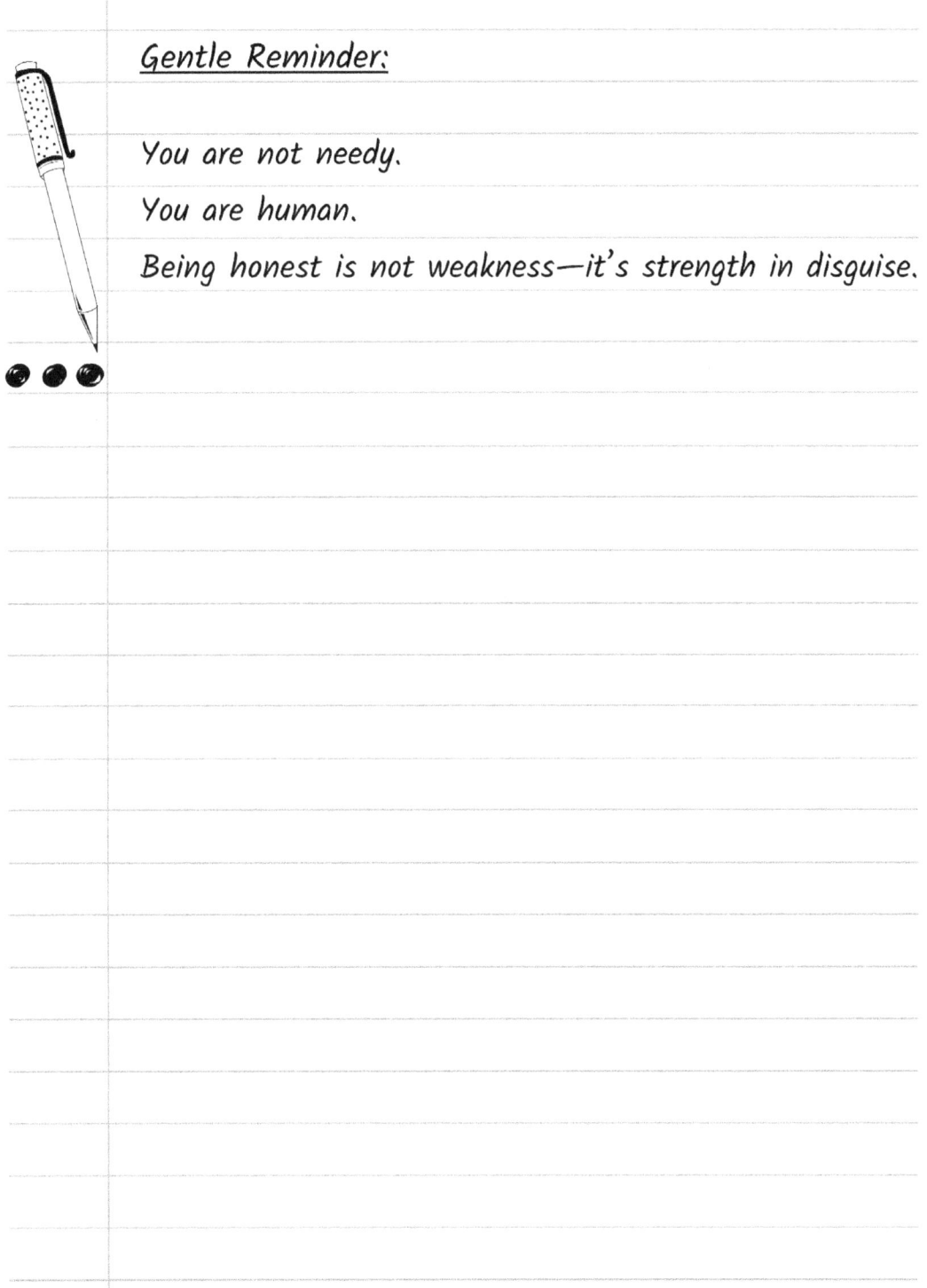

Gentle Reminder:

You are not needy.

You are human.

Being honest is not weakness—it's strength in disguise.

Let's look at the example of how Jessica found authentic love.

JESSICA'S JOURNEY TO AUTHENTIC LOVE

At 32, Jessica felt like she'd been on this merry-go-round forever. Every relationship started with excitement but ended in heartbreak. She was tired of pretending to be someone she wasn't just to keep a partner interested.

One rainy Sunday, curled up with a cup of tea, Jessica stumbled upon an article about attachment styles. The description of anxious attachment fit her perfectly. She always worried her partners would leave, constantly sought reassurance, and often felt overwhelmed by her emotions in relationships.

This discovery sparked something in Jessica. She decided it was time for a change. Over the next few months, she threw herself into self-improvement. She started therapy, read books on attachment, and spent time journaling about her past relationships.

Slowly but surely, Jessica began to understand herself better. She realized how her fear of abandonment stemmed from her childhood experiences. She learned to recognize her anxious behaviors and found healthier ways to cope with her emotions.

The biggest challenge came when Jessica decided to start dating again. This time, she was determined to be honest about who she was. On her first date with Mark, she took a deep breath and shared that she was working on her anxious attachment style.

To her surprise, Mark didn't run away. Instead, he appreciated her honesty and opened up about his own journey of personal growth. Their conversation flowed easily, touching on hopes, fears, and past experiences.

As they continued to see each other, Jessica practiced being true to herself. When she felt the urge to bombard Mark with texts, she paused and reminded herself that it was okay to give him space. When she needed reassurance, she learned to ask for it directly instead of hinting or getting upset.

It wasn't always easy. There were moments when Jessica's old insecurities bubbled up. But instead of letting them control her, she talked to Mark about her feelings. Together, they found ways to make each other feel secure while respecting boundaries.

For the first time, Jessica felt like she could be herself in a relationship. She didn't have to pretend to be more independent than she was or hide her need for closeness. Being authentic made her feel more confident and secure.

As months passed, Jessica realized she was in the healthiest relationship of her life. She and Mark supported each other's growth, communicated openly, and built a strong foundation of trust.

Looking back, Jessica could hardly believe how far she'd come. By embracing her true self and doing the work to heal, she had finally found the authentic love she'd always dreamed of. She knew there would still be challenges ahead, but she felt ready to face them—not alone, but with a partner who accepted her, anxious attachment and all.

KEY TAKEAWAYS

- This chapter outlines signs of readiness for authentic love, including awareness of one's attachment style, trust in the recovery process, feeling safe alone and with others, and improved emotional reactions.

- This chapter also provides guidance on choosing a partner after personal growth, suggesting learning from past mistakes, looking for partners with secure attachments or those actively working on themselves, and emphasizing the importance of being intentional in relationship choices.

- It stresses the importance of being authentic in relationships, particularly for those with anxious attachment styles.

148

BONUS CHAPTER

BUILDING A STRONGER YOU—TIPS FOR POST-RECOVERY SUCCESS

Now, we offer you some practical tools to help shift your attachment style toward a more secure one. Remember, this isn't about quick fixes or becoming perfect. It's about gradual, meaningful progress.

These tips are like a toolbox—you don't need to use every tool at once. Experiment, find what works for you, and keep practicing. It's important to be patient with yourself, as it can take a while to learn and grow. This journey might bring up challenging emotions, and that's okay. Be gentle with yourself, and seek support when you need it.

LEARN FROM OTHERS WITH SECURE ATTACHMENT

Think of securely attached people as your attachment style role models. They're like the chill, confident friends who always seem to have their relationships figured out. The thing is, they learned that behavior, and so can you.

Start by observing how securely attached people handle relationship situations. When their partner is busy and can't respond right away, do they panic? No, they trust that everything's fine and get on with their day. When they need something, do they hint and hope their partner will guess? No, they ask directly and clearly.

Now, here's where it gets practical. Next time you're in a tricky relationship situation, pause and ask yourself: "What would a securely attached person do here?" Maybe instead of sending a flurry of anxious texts when your partner is late, you'd take a deep breath and assume they're just stuck in traffic. Or instead of silently stewing when your needs aren't met, you'd have an open, calm conversation about it.

Compare these secure behaviors to your own. Where do you see differences? These are your growth opportunities. Maybe you need to work on trusting your partner more or expressing your needs more directly.

Remember, this isn't about beating yourself up for not being "secure enough." It's about learning and growing. Each time you notice a difference and make a small change, you rewire your attachment style.

Pick one secure behavior to focus on this week. Maybe it's not checking your phone constantly when waiting for a text or speaking up about something that bothers you instead of letting it simmer. Practice it consciously. It might initially feel weird, but you're learning a new skill.

By regularly practicing these secure behaviors, you're not just copying them—you're gradually internalizing a more secure attachment style. It's like learning any new habit: With time and practice, it becomes more natural.

EXPRESSING YOUR NEEDS AND EMOTIONS AUTHENTICALLY

This is really important, especially if you've been feeling nervous or clingy in relationships.

First, focus on you. Think about what you want to achieve, just for yourself. Maybe you want to learn a new hobby, get better at your job, or even solve a tricky puzzle. When you set these personal goals and work toward them, it's like giving yourself a high-five. It feels great when you realize just how capable you are.

It can be difficult to talk about your feelings. One way of doing it is to imagine your emotions are like different colored balloons inside you. Instead of holding them all in until you burst, try letting them out one by one.

Here's how you might do it:

- If you're feeling sad, you could say, "I'm feeling pretty down right now."

- If you're jealous, try, "When I saw that, I felt a bit jealous."

- If you're worried, you might say, "I'm a little anxious about this situation."

It's okay to ask for what you need. If you want a hug, it's alright to say, "I could really use a hug right now." That's not being needy; it's being honest.

At first, it might feel awkward or scary to open up, but the more you practice, the easier it gets. The cool part is, when you're honest about your feelings, it often brings you closer to people.

By working on yourself and expressing your feelings, you're building a stronger, more confident you. It's like growing roots that help you stand tall on your own while still connecting with others in a healthy way.

HEALING BY DREAMING

Let's talk about healing and dreaming, especially for folks who worry a lot about their relationships. It's like you're always checking your phone, wondering if your partner still cares. Sound familiar?

When you're always focused on someone else, it's easy to forget about yourself. It's like you've been watching someone else's movie instead of starring in your own. You need to start acting like the main character in your own life story.

Dreaming isn't just for bedtime. It's about imagining a future that excites you. Maybe you've been so busy worrying about your relationship that you forgot to think about what you want. It's possible to fix this.

Here's a little story about dreaming:

Imagine you're in a big field. For a long time, you've been standing in one spot, watching the clouds and hoping they'll form the shapes you want. You decide to walk around. You find a nice hill and climb it. Suddenly, you can see so much more. There are flowers you never noticed, paths you could explore, even a little stream in the distance. That's what dreaming is like. It's seeing all the possibilities in your life.

So, let's practice dreaming:

- What would you do if you weren't worried about anyone else?

- Is there a place you've always wanted to visit?

- What's a skill you'd love to learn?

Write these dreams down. They don't have to be big—maybe you want to try a new hairstyle or learn to cook your favorite dish. The important thing is that these dreams are yours.

Now, here's the cool part: As you start focusing on your dreams, you might find that you worry less about your relationships. You're building a life that makes you happy, with or without someone else.

It's okay to care about others, but don't forget to care about yourself too. Your dreams matter. By working on them, you're not just healing—you're growing into the person you're meant to be.

HEALING BY DREAMING

A guided practice for anxious hearts

Do you spend a lot of time worrying about your relationships?

Checking your phone... waiting for a reply... wondering if you're still loved?

You're not alone. But it's time to shift the spotlight back to you.

Healing begins when you start dreaming again.

Not just daydreaming—but imagining a future that feels exciting and yours.

Step 1: Remember, You're the Main Character

When your energy is always wrapped around someone else, it's like you're watching their movie—forgetting that you're the star of your own.

Take a moment. Breathe. Bring the focus back to you.

Step 2: A Dreaming Visualization

Imagine this: You're standing in an open field. For a long time, you've stared at the sky, hoping the clouds will turn into what you want.

But today, you start walking. You climb a small hill... and suddenly, you see more. Flowers you never noticed. Paths leading in new directions. A sparkling stream in the distance.

This is dreaming—not fantasy, but perspective. When you move, when you dream, your life opens up.

Step 3: Your Dream List

Let's get practical. Don't worry about whether it's realistic. This is about permission to want again.

→ What would you do if you weren't worrying about anyone else?

→ A place you've always wanted to visit:

→ A skill you'd love to learn:

→ A little dream that brings you joy (a haircut, a hobby, a recipe?)

Step 4: Why This Matters

The more you focus on your own dreams, the less power anxiety has over you.

You're not just waiting for love—you're creating a life you love.

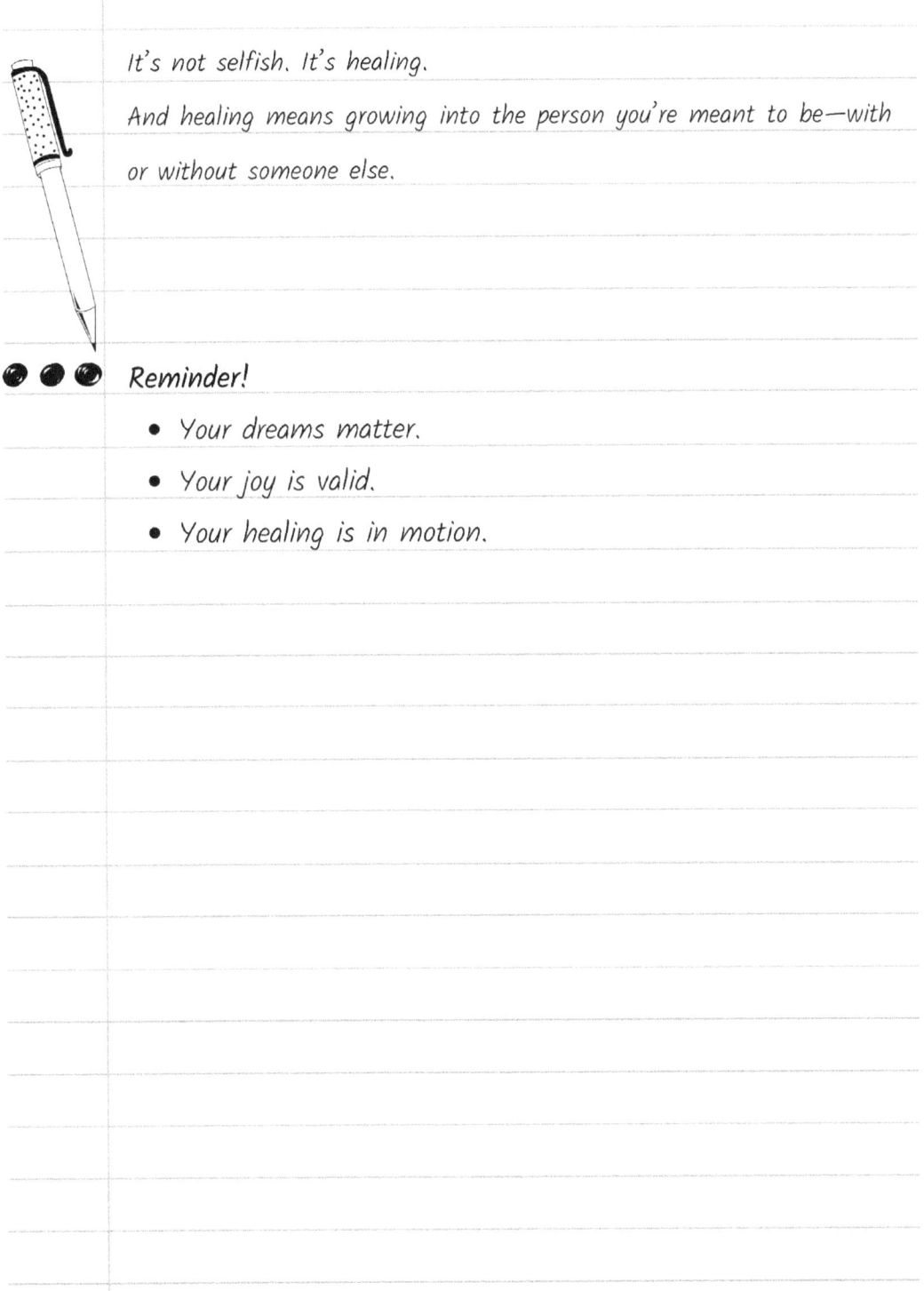

It's not selfish. It's healing.

And healing means growing into the person you're meant to be—with or without someone else.

Reminder!

- Your dreams matter.
- Your joy is valid.
- Your healing is in motion.

PRACTICING DAILY DETACHMENT

Letting go is almost like loosening your grip on a balloon string—you're still holding it, but you're not squeezing so tight your knuckles turn white.

You know that feeling when you're so worried about someone or something that it's all you can think about? Like when you're waiting for a text back and you keep checking your phone every two seconds? That's what we're trying to ease up on.

Detachment doesn't mean you stop caring. It's more like taking a step back so you can see the whole picture. Imagine you're watching a movie. If you sit too close to the screen, everything's blurry. When you move back a bit, suddenly everything's clear.

Here's how you can practice this every day:

- Start your morning with a little pep talk. You can say things like:

"How others treat me says more about them than me."

"Things will work out, even if it's not how I expect."

"I'm okay with whatever happens today."

- When you feel yourself getting worked up, take a deep breath and remind yourself:

"I can handle this."

"I'm going to focus on what I can control."

"I'm thankful for [something good in your life]."

Do something just for you each day. Maybe it's reading a book, going for a walk, or trying a new recipe. This helps remind you that you're a whole person on your own.

When you catch yourself obsessing over something, gently redirect your thoughts. It's like changing the channel on a TV.

By practicing detachment, you're giving yourself more freedom. You're saying, "I trust myself to handle whatever comes my way." Slowly, you'll find yourself feeling stronger and more at peace.

THERAPY

Sometimes you may need extra help on your journey. Think of a therapist as a friendly guide who can help you figure out where you are, where you want to go, and how to get there. Especially when it comes to dealing with those worried, clingy feelings in relationships.

Now, I know what you might be thinking: *Therapy? Isn't that for people with "real" problems?* If something's bugging you, it's real enough. You don't need to be in a crisis to benefit from therapy.

Therapy can give you the following:

- It can offer a safe place to talk about your feelings without worrying about being judged.

- You'll learn new ways to handle stress and anxiety. It's like getting new tools for your emotional toolbox.

- A therapist can help you spot patterns in your relationships that you might not see on your own.

- You'll practice healthier ways of thinking and behaving. It's like rehearsing for real life.

Ask your doctor to recommend a therapist, as they often have connections with mental health professionals. If you're employed or attending school, it's worth checking whether your workplace or educational institution offers counseling services, as these can be convenient and cost-effective options. You could search online for therapists in your local area who specialize in attachment issues. This method allows you to find professionals with expertise tailored to your specific needs.

It's okay to shop around. If the first therapist doesn't feel right, try another. It's like finding a good pair of shoes—sometimes you need to try a few before you find the perfect fit.

Going to therapy doesn't mean you're broken or weak. Actually, it takes a lot of strength to ask for help. It's a sign that you're taking charge of your life and your happiness.

So, if you're feeling stuck or overwhelmed, consider giving therapy a try. You deserve to feel better, and a good therapist can help you get there.

THERAPY: A STEP TOWARD HEALING

Sometimes, extra support can make all the difference. Think of therapy as a safe space—a supportive conversation with someone trained to help you sort through your thoughts, recognize patterns, and move forward in healthier ways.

What Can Therapy Offer You?

- A judgment-free zone where you can speak openly and honestly;
- Practical tools to manage anxiety, stress, and overwhelming emotions;
- Insight into relationship patterns you might not notice alone;
- A space to practice healthier thinking and behavior, like emotional rehearsal for life;

Is Therapy Right for You?

You don't need to be in crisis to benefit. If something's bothering you, it's real enough.

Take a moment and ask yourself:

→ What have I been struggling with lately?

→ Would it help to talk to someone who won't judge or interrupt me?

→ Am I tired of repeating the same patterns in relationships?

How to Start Looking for a Therapist?

Try one or more of these options:

- Ask your doctor for a referral;
- Check if your school or workplace offers counseling;
- Search online for therapists who specialize in attachment issues or relationship concerns;
- Don't be afraid to shop around—it's okay if the first one isn't a perfect fit.

A Note to Remember:

"Going to therapy doesn't mean you're broken. It means you're brave enough to want something better."

Self-Reflection Prompt

→ If therapy could help one area of your life feel lighter, what would it be?

PAY ATTENTION TO PROTEST BEHAVIOR

Even grown-ups in relationships can throw tantrums when they don't get what they want. When we're feeling anxious or insecure, sometimes we do things that aren't helpful. It's like our heart is screaming, "Pay attention to me!" but it comes out all wrong.

This behavior might show up in different ways. You might find yourself constantly texting or calling someone or suddenly going quiet to see if they'll chase after you. Maybe you're keeping score of every little thing they did wrong or getting angry for no real reason. Some people might threaten to leave the relationship just to see how their partner reacts or try to manipulate situations to get what they want. Another common tactic is trying to make your partner jealous by flirting with others or talking about exes.

These behaviors might feel like they're helping in the moment, but they usually make things worse by pushing people away. Do your best to notice this type of behavior, and work on changing it. Just being aware is already a big first step. Then, take a deep breath and give yourself a moment before you react. Ask yourself, "What am I feeling? What do I really need?"

Try to express your feelings clearly and calmly. Instead of acting out, you could say, "I'm feeling anxious and I could use some reassurance." Remember, it's okay to have needs. However, it's important to express them in a healthy way.

Learning to spot and change these behaviors takes time and practice. Be patient with yourself. Each time you choose a healthier way to express yourself, you're building a stronger, more secure you. That's something to be proud of.

HEARTFELT WORDS FROM A THERAPIST

Think of learning new habits like riding a bike. Remember how many times you fell before you finally got the hang of it? That's what changing your thoughts and behaviors is like. It takes practice, and yes, sometimes it feels like you're hearing the same thing over and over.

Just like you wouldn't expect to ride a bike perfectly after trying once, you can't expect to change old habits overnight. It's all about repetition. It's like when you're learning a new song—you sing it again and again until it sticks in your head.

Now, I've sat across from lots of people in therapy, and at first, I thought I was some kind of wizard making magic happen. The real magic comes from the people themselves. They're the ones doing the hard work, repeating the good stuff until it becomes second nature.

There's this saying I love: "Yesterday's shower won't wash today's dirt" (The Coaching Masters, 2024). It's a funny way of saying that you need to keep at it, day after day. Just because you had a good day yesterday doesn't mean you can skip the work today.

So, if you're feeling frustrated because you're hearing the same advice again and again, remember: That's how change happens. It's like watering a plant. You don't just water it once and expect it to grow. You do it every day, even when you can't see the changes happening underground.

Keep practicing those new thoughts and behaviors. They might feel awkward at first, but so did riding a bike. Look at you now0151—you can probably ride without even thinking about it. That's the goal with these new habits too, so don't give up.

KEY TAKEAWAYS

- This chapter emphasizes the importance of self-focus and personal growth, encouraging readers to pursue their own dreams and goals as a way to reduce relationship anxiety and build self-confidence.

- It highlights the importance of recognizing and addressing "protest behaviors" in relationships, which are unhelpful reactions stemming from anxiety and insecurity.

CONCLUSION

As we come to the end of this journey, let's take a moment to reflect on how far you have come. Remember that scenario we opened with? The one where you were anxiously checking your phone, spiraling into worry over an unanswered text? Take a deep breath and imagine how you might handle that situation now.

Perhaps you'd still feel a twinge of anxiety—that's normal and human. However, now you have the tools to recognize that feeling for what it is. You can ground yourself in the present moment, challenge those anxious thoughts, and respond from a place of self-assurance rather than fear. That's growth. That's healing.

Throughout this book, we have explored the roots of anxious attachment, delving into the science behind how our early experiences shape our adult relationships. We have examined how anxious attachment manifests in daily life, from the constant need for reassurance to the fear of abandonment that can overshadow even the happiest moments.

More importantly, we have armed you with practical strategies to manage these anxious thoughts and behaviors. You have learned techniques for self-soothing, for building self-esteem, and for setting healthy boundaries. You have discovered how to communicate your needs effectively and how to navigate conflicts in a way that strengthens rather than threatens your relationships.

Remember, the goal was never to eliminate anxiety entirely. Anxiety, in moderate doses, serves a purpose. It can alert us to potential threats and motivate us to address issues in our relationships. What we have aimed for is a shift from anxious to secure attachment— a state where you can feel generally safe and confident in your relationships while having the tools to manage anxiety when it does arise.

This journey toward secure attachment is ongoing. There may still be moments when old patterns resurface, when insecurity creeps in, or when you find yourself slipping into anxious behaviors. That's okay. Healing isn't linear, and setbacks are a normal part of the process. What matters is how you respond to these moments. Now, you have the awareness to recognize what's happening and the tools to course correct.

As you move forward, remember to be patient and compassionate with yourself. It will take time and effort to change long-standing, entrenched patterns. Every time you choose self-soothing over spiraling, every time you communicate a need clearly instead of hoping your partner will read your mind, every time you set a healthy boundary—these are all victories worth acknowledging.

Continue to practice the techniques you've learned. Like any skill, secure attachment gets stronger with use. Keep working on building a fulfilling life outside of your romantic relationships. Nurture your friendships, pursue your passions, and continue to grow as an individual. Remember, the most secure relationships are formed between two whole, independent people who choose to be together, not out of need but out of want.

If you're currently in a relationship, you may have noticed changes as you've worked through this book. As you have become more secure within yourself, you may find your relationship dynamics shifting in positive ways. Continue to communicate openly with your partner about your journey. Invite them to learn and grow with you.

If you're single, you're now better equipped to enter your next relationship from a place of security and self-awareness. You know what healthy love looks like, and you're prepared to both give and receive it.

Remember that seeking additional support is always an option. Whether through therapy, support groups, or continued self-help work, there are many resources available to support your ongoing growth.

As we close this book, I want you to know how proud you should be of yourself. Taking this step to understand and heal your attachment style is no small feat. It takes courage to look inward, to confront painful patterns, and to commit to change. You have done that. You have taken the first and most important steps on the path to secure attachment.

Imagine for a moment the possibilities that lie ahead. Relationships where you feel safe and valued. A strong sense of self-worth that doesn't depend on constant external validation. The ability to give and receive love freely, without the shadow of fear. This is all within your reach.

You started this book seeking to understand and heal your anxious attachment. You're ending it with a toolbox full of strategies, a deeper understanding of yourself, and a road map for continued growth. The journey doesn't end here; in many ways, it's just beginning. You're now prepared and empowered. You're on your way to secure attachment and the fulfilling relationships you deserve.

So, as you close this book, take a deep breath. Feel the strength within you. You're no longer at the mercy of anxious attachment. You're the author of your own story, and a new chapter is just beginning. Step forward with confidence, with hope, and with the knowledge that you are capable of secure, loving relationships. Your journey to secure attachment continues, and the best is yet to come.

SCAN THE QR CODE TO LEAVE YOUR HONEST REVIEW

If this material was helpful to you, I would be very grateful to you if you will share it with your friends or with someone you know who needs it.

Also, in order for me to improve things in the future, you can share your honest opinion by leaving a sincere review.

It truly means a lot to me!

Simply scan this QR code to do just that!

REFERENCES

Ackerman, C. (2024a, September 20). *What is self-regulation? (+95 skills and strategies).* PositivePsychology.com. https://positivepsychology.com/self-regulation/

Ackerman, C. E. (2024b, September 26). *What is attachment theory? Bowlby's 4 stages explained.* Positive Psychology.com. https://positivepsychology.com/attachment-theory/

Arlin, C. (2023, September 19). *Autogenic training for reducing anxiety.* Verywell Mind. https://www.verywellmind.com/how-to-practice-autogenic-training-for-relaxation-3024387

The Attachment Project. (2024, July 10). *What is attachment theory?* The Attachment Project. https://www.attachmentproject.com/attachment-theory/

Autogenic training. (n.d.). VA Office of Patient Centered Care and Cultural Transformation. https://www.va.gov/WHOLEHEALTHLIBRARY/docs/Autogenic-Training.pdf

Brooten-Brooks, M. C. (2024, July 16). *How to set healthy boundaries with anyone.* Verywell Health. https://www.verywellhealth.com/setting-boundaries-5208802

Burton, N. (2024, June 23). *The 10 golden rules of communication.* Psychology Today. https://www.psychologytoday.com/za/blog/hide-and-seek/201207/the-10-golden-rules-of-communication

Chelsea Psychology Clinic. (2022, November 9). *What are my needs? Identifying your emotional needs in a relationship.* Chelsea Psychology Clinic.

https://www.thechelseapsychologyclinic.com/sex-relationships/what-are-my-needs/

Cherry, K. (2023a, February 22). *What is attachment theory?* Verywell Mind. https://www.verywellmind.com/what-is-attachment-theory-2795337

Cherry, K. (2023b, May 4). *The power of positive thinking*. Verywell Mind. https://www.verywellmind.com/what-is-positive-thinking-2794772

The Coaching Masters. (2024, October 4). *Yesterday's shower isn't going to keep you clean today*. The Coaching Masters. https://thecoachingmasters.com/yesterdays-shower-isnt-going-to-keep-you-clean-today/

Crowell, J. A., Treboux, D., & Waters, E. (1999). The adult attachment interview and the relationship questionnaire: Relations to reports of mothers and partners. *Personal Relationships*, 6(1), 1–18. https://doi.org/10.1111/j.1475-6811.1999.tb00208.x

David, S. (2022, October 12). *Emotional pyramid of needs*. Susan David. https://www.susandavid.com/resource/emotional-pyramid-of-needs/

Emerson, M. S. (2024, January 8). *8 ways you can improve your communication skills*. Professional Development | Harvard DCE. https://professional.dce.harvard.edu/blog/8-ways-you-can-improve-your-communication-skills/

Emma. (2024, October 10). *How to meet your own emotional needs through self-validation*. Joy Ninja. https://joyninja.com/how-to-meet-your-own-emotional-needs/

Gattig, N. (2024, September 25). 18 effective strategies to improve your communication skills. *BetterUp*. https://www.betterup.com/blog/effective-strategies-to-improve-your-communication-skills

Gornall, L. (2024, September 27). *Toxic people: 9 signs a person is toxic – and what to do about it*. Red Online. https://www.redonline.co.uk/wellbeing/a28577908/signs-a-person-is-toxic/

Gupta, S. (2024, April 18). *What does secure attachment look and feel like? Plus how to develop it*. Verywell Mind. https://www.verywellmind.com/secure-attachment-signs-benefits-and-how-to-cultivate-it-8628802

Hanson, M. (2021, January 9). *The psychology of setting motivating and satisfying goals*. Outside Online. https://www.outsideonline.com/health/running/culture/the-psychology-of-setting-motivating-and-satisfying-goals/

Harbinger, J. (2022, April 25). *8 Signs it's time to cut a toxic person out of your life (and how to do it)*. Jordan Harbinger. https://www.jordanharbinger.com/8-signs-its-time-to-cut-a-toxic-person-out-of-your-life-and-how-to-do-it/

Lindberg, S. (2019, November 22). *What to know about autogenic training*. Healthline. https://www.healthline.com/health/mental-health/autogenic-training

Mandriota, M. (2021, October 14). *Here is how to identify your attachment style*. Psych Central. https://psychcentral.com/health/4-attachment-styles-in-relationships

Pattemore, C. (2021, June 3). *10 ways to build and preserve better boundaries*. Psych Central. https://psychcentral.com/lib/10-way-to-build-and-preserve-better-boundaries

Pennelle, O. (2020, March 25). *The power of mastering your own mind*. Shondaland. https://www.shondaland.com/live/body/a31816571/the-power-of-mastering-your-own-mind/

Perry, E. (2022a, April 12). Improve your life with a new outlook: 10 benefits of positive thinking. *BetterUp*. https://www.betterup.com/blog/positive-thinking-benefits

Perry, E. (2022b, August 5). A guide for using motivation to achieve goals. *BetterUp*. https://www.betterup.com/blog/how-motivation-helps-in-achieving-goals

Raypole, C. (2019, November 21). *Do's and don'ts for dealing with toxic behavior*. Healthline. https://www.healthline.com/health/how-to-deal-with-toxic-people

Raypole, C. (2021, October 21). *10 emotional needs to consider in relationships*. Healthline. https://www.healthline.com/health/emotional-needs

Reid, S. (2024, August 21). *Setting healthy boundaries in relationships*. HelpGuide.org. https://www.helpguide.org/relationships/social-connection/setting-healthy-boundaries-in-relationships

Robinson, L., Segal, J., & Smith, M. (2024, September 25). *Effective communication: Improving your interpersonal skills*. HelpGuide.org. https://www.helpguide.org/relationships/communication/effective-communication

Sanok, J. (2022, April 14). *A guide to setting better boundaries*. Harvard Business Review. https://hbr.org/2022/04/a-guide-to-setting-better-boundaries

Whelan, C. (2022, September 30). *What is emotional self-regulation and how do you develop it?* Healthline. https://www.healthline.com/health/emotional-self-regulation

Young, K. (2024, April 8). *Toxic people: 12 things they go and how to deal with them*. Heysigmund.com. https://www.heysigmund.com/toxic-people/